RIDE
OF YOUR
LIFE

LYN ST. JAMES

RIDE
OF YOUR
LIFE

A Race Car Driver's
Journey

New York

I'd like to dedicate this book to five people who contributed significantly to my life and career, yet are no longer with us. It takes special people who are willing to share their knowledge and experience to make one's life move forward, and these gentlemen did that for me in so many ways. While illnesses took their lives, I know they also contributed to others who would want people to know just how special they were.

Thank you John Carusso, Art Schultz, Dan Marisi, Walter Hayes, and Tom Binford.

VI

ACKNOWLEDGMENTS

I want to thank Karlene Pinkney for teaching me to be an athlete and competitor and for being a lifelong friend; John Carusso for teaching me to dream and follow my passions, and for letting go; Walter Hayes for having the vision to see my talents and abilities and for mentoring me along the way at Ford Motor Company; Michael Kranefuss for teaching me to be tough; David Scott for teaching me that there are men who listen to women and who appreciate their contributions; Don Courtney for teaching me to believe in myself and to concentrate on the doughnut and not the hole; Art Schultz for teaching me that racing was a means to an end and not the end in itself; Rolland Todd for teaching me about possibilities, opportunities, and empowerment; Dick Simon for giving me the opportunity of a lifetime and making it happen; Dane Miller for saying yes; Emory Donaldson for answering so many questions and reminding me to laugh; John Mecom for opening his heart and his family to me and for providing a place for me to dream about driving at Indy; John Gorsline for teaching me how to have fun; my friends at the Women's Sports Foundation for teaching me to take pride in being a female athlete and showing me the way to give back; Sheila Plank for reminding me that I was a lady; Kai Binford for being such a beautiful role model and dear soul; Deb Turner for being so happy; Trish Moran for always being there, helmet ready to go; Michelle Marquis for helping me do the things I want to do for others; Markie Lyons for fulfilling my vision that there will someday be a Jessica Gordon; Sara Senske for making me realize that I may not be the first woman to win the Indy 500; my daughter, Lindsay Lessman, for teaching me unconditional love; my mother for teaching me to drive and to "listen to your car because it gives you warnings and signals" and to realize that we can never judge others because we haven't walked in their shoes; Dan Marisi for teaching me so much about mental discipline; Nick, Frank, and Jacques for teaching me how to train my uncooperative body; and to so many crew members (too many to name, but you know who you are) who taught me so much about myself and the sport of racing. Without the incredible group of individuals that I've been blessed to have on my team over the years I know there is no way I would have been able to take the green and checkered flags and cope with the yellow and black flags, both on the racetrack and in life. Thank you.

To the Simon family, you know how I feel about you, and there are no more words to express the love and respect I have for you all, and to John, Emmanuel, Steve, Gary, Richee, Justin, and everyone else I named in these pages, I can't thank you enough.

Thanks, too, to Mark Reiter at IMG Literary, Gretchen Young and Will Schwalbe at Hyperion, and Larry Schatz for believing in this project and seeing it through to the end. And a huge thanks to Steve Eubanks for his enthusiasm, interest, and great writing.

And to all the others who contributed in both small and big ways to this book and to my career as an Indy car driver, I want to offer my heartfelt thanks. You're the reason this book exists. I hope you are as proud of it as I am.

CONTENTS

INTRODUCTION

WHAT IT'S LIKE   1 to pg. 12 = (12 pgs)

ONE

chpt. 1   **DRIVE THE COURSE YOU'RE GIVEN**   13 to 28 = (16 pgs)

TWO

chpt. 2   **MAKING IT HAPPEN**   29 to 44 = (16 pgs)

THREE

chpt 3   **YOU NEVER KNOW TILL YOU ASK**   45 to 62 = (18 pgs)

FOUR

chpt 4   **TEAM SPIRIT**   63 to 86 = 24 pgs

FIVE

chpt 5   **THE WILL TO PREPARE TO WIN**   87 to 98 = 12 pgs.

CONTENTS

SIX

Chpt. 6 – SEAT TIME   99 to 116 = 18 pgs

SEVEN

chpt 7 – FIRST RIDE   117 to 134 = 18 pgs

EIGHT

Chpt 8 – IN THE BLINK OF AN EYE   135 to 162 = (28 pgs)

NINE

chpt 9 – PRESSING AHEAD   163 to 182 = (20 pgs)

TEN

Chpt. 10 – THE GRIND TO BUMP   183 to 196 = (14 pgs)

ELEVEN

Chpt 11 – CONTROLLING YOUR MOMENT   197 to 208 = (12 pgs)

TWELVE

chpt 12 – MAKING THE SHOW   209 to 230 = (22 pgs)

THIRTEEN

Chpt. 13 – THE GLORY OF TEAMWORK   231 to 240 = (10 pgs)

FOURTEEN

Chpt 14 – LADIES AND GENTLEMEN   241 to 260 = (20 pgs)

FIFTEEN

Chpt. 15 – LAST LAPS/NEXT LAPS   261 to 274 = (14 pgs)

Alloyed within

> *Rare earth's indeed.*

Grace

> *Strength*

>> *Honesty*

>>> *Form Lyn*

Clay, life fired, to beauty

Shared with those she passes.

—C. MICHAEL POWELL, 1982

XIV.

Photo: Courtesy of Tony Di Zinno

ges from pg 1 to pg 12 =(12 pgs)

WHAT IT'S LIKE

There's no sound in the world like the scream of an Indy car. The seamless vibrato of an eight-cylinder engine humming at over 10,000 rpms and the nerve-racking pitch change as an open-wheel race car flies by at 200 mph are sounds everybody knows. Even those who don't follow racing can identify the tenor of an Indy car, which is why television uses an audio teaser to promote the network's telecast of the Indy 500. Why show pictures when two seconds of sound will do the trick?

The sounds are a little different when you're sitting behind the wheel, staring out over the cylindrical nose cone with two large racing tires in your peripheral vision. For starters, the motor is about six inches behind your head, which means you feel the sound as much as you hear it. Because you're in the car, you don't experience the Doppler effect when the car moves past you. You're wearing molded earplugs, which act as both a muffler and a means of communicating with your crew, and you have plenty of insulation. A fire-retardant hood called a balaclava that resembles a ski mask covers most of your face, including your ears, and the helmet—a sleek, aerodynamic work of art with a dozen different functions, not the least of which is to save your life if you get into trouble—provides another two inches of padding around your ears, but the sound isn't blocked out: not by a long shot. Sitting in the custom-molded race seat a few inches off the ground, the most dominant sound you hear is a constant high-pitched wail, a noise that is at once as beautiful as a concert piano and as unnerving as a sonic boom.

I've been racing for most of my adult life, having driven in seven Indy 500s and, before that, racing sports cars and setting a number of national and international speed records in a Ford Probe and then a Ford Thunderbird, and I've never grown tired of the sounds, the smell, or the atmosphere of a racetrack. My heart rate quickens when I drive through the gates and hear the familiar noises, wrenches banging against concrete, air guns loosening and tightening lug nuts, and the explosive cries of engines being tested and retested. They are all like songbirds.

The Indianapolis Motor Speedway, one of the oldest and largest racetracks in the world and the home to the biggest spectator sporting event on the planet, has its own unique sounds, which I've also grown to love. There is the squeal of police whistles being blown with great enthusiasm by the security staff, known as Yellow Shirts for their distinctive attire, and the throaty patter of motorized golf carts zipping back and forth between Gasoline Alley and pit lane. The crowd sounds are different at Indy as well. Unlike other race-tracks, which are usually located far from the city limits, the Speedway is located six miles from downtown and is a part of Indianapolis's culture and history, and the knowledgeable and appreciative crowds reflect that. Drivers are cheered wherever they go in Indy. I often have people yelling, "Go get 'em, Lyn," as I wander through the grocery store in blue jeans and sun-glasses. The cheers are great; the recognition is great; even the silence is great. There's nothing in the world like the eerie hush that follows a crash at Indy as 400,000 spectators hold their collective breath and wait for the driver to crawl from the wreckage and wave to the crowd. To the novice, racing might seem noisy, an unnerving high-decibel cadence. But to me the auditory experience is as sweet and inviting as a sum-mer concert.

I only wish I could spend more time listening. As an Indy car driver, I'm away from the track more than I'm on it. I give seminars and speeches, attend sponsor meetings, and make appearances at functions around the country. Like many driv-ers, I'm an independent contractor and able to decide when and where I appear. That means I'm free to do as few or as many appearances as I wish to negotiate. I choose to do more rather than less, because I love sharing my passion and I've found that the lessons I've learned in racing apply to everyday life as much as they do to racing.

When I'm on the road, the question I'm asked more than any other is, "How does it feel to drive a race car?" That's usually followed by something more specific like, "Are you scared?" or "What goes through your mind when you're driving?" These are natural questions. Speed has always fascinated people, and the concept of driving a car in excess of 200 mph is something the general populace cannot fathom. Most people over age sixteen spend a considerable amount of time driving cars, but that experience doesn't explain the feeling of racing. Instead it only adds to the mystique. People understand the principles of driving; they just can't imagine doing it at racing speeds.

I try to convey the feelings of racing, but it's difficult to paint the complete picture in words. The ritual begins with putting on your race suit, which is made up of two layers of fire-retardant clothing, an inner layer similar to thermal underwear and a thick outer layer that looks and feels like a flight suit. It's designed to fit snugly around your body, and every stitch of clothing is made of Nomex, a fire-retardant fiber manufactured by DuPont, or a combination of Nomex and Kevlar, the same material used in bulletproof vests. Even your socks, boots, and underwear are Nomex. You're also wearing gloves; not fashionable leather driving gloves like you see in old James Bond movies, but thick Nomex and leather gloves that look bulky. Believe it or not, all of this is really more comfortable than it looks because it's custom-fitted and becomes like a suit of armor. The only item that doesn't contain Nomex is the Kevlar helmet you're wearing, and the only

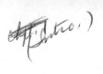

unclothed portion of your body is the area around your eyes, and that is covered by the helmet's visor.

When I strap myself into the race car, it's as if I'm becoming one with the car and stepping into my final layer of clothing. I actually feel like I'm "wearing" the car. Instead of my body being the border of my power, the car now becomes an extension of me. And when that car has more than 600 horsepower and can exceed 220 mph, that's extreme power that I now have. Everything is connected—the car and I are not separate things. My mind and body are totally tuned in to the moment and everything is clear, almost like driving in a tunnel where all the action ahead is very clear but the things outside the tunnel are blurred. It's a feeling of absolute power. A sense of joy and elation arise from the feeling of complete harmony when the car is set up right. Everything seems to happen with unusual ease and precision, "almost by itself." Nothing else, no other thought, interferes with the total focus on the present. You cannot think of anything else other than the feel of the car and the action of the race at the moment. When I'm driving the car, I get into a rhythm, a flow of movement that happens almost automatically. Prior to the race, there is a movement "frequency" of the body that is evident in my speech pattern, body movements, and mental agility; all at a heightened level. People around me say this is noticeable. We call it my "race face." Just as an electric current passes through a power line to light a fixture at a frequency of 60 Hz, so does my body experience an electrochemical change. The adrenal glands activate and my neural-electrical frequency varies according to the perceived and real demands placed on my system.

If I'm driving on a particular day I try to suit up an hour or so before we're scheduled to be on the track. This gives me plenty of time to get comfortable in my racing suit and prepare myself mentally for the day ahead. The atmosphere at the track is different on days that cars are running. There's a palpable sense of urgency as people scurry around the garages. The smell of methanol wafts through the open air, burning your eyes and nostrils the way an open bottle of ammonia does when left in an unventilated room. Drivers and mechanics are accustomed to the smells, and after a while we don't even notice them. Nor do we pay a lot of attention to what's happening in other garages. During one practice session at Indy a fistfight broke out in one of the garages, and the mechanics in the bay next door didn't even look up. Everyone is focused when cars are on the track. Distractions are unacceptable.

Most people I speak to are surprised when I say that I don't feel any emotion once I crawl into the tub of the race car. I don't experience emotions because I become one with the car and "feel" only what the car feels. An Indy car goes from 0 to 100 mph in less than three seconds, and the g-forces we pull through turns are about the same as those experienced by the space shuttle crews during blastoff. The only time I've felt more g-forces than when driving an Indy car was when I flew with the Thunderbirds and Blue Angels at over 9 g's. And it's different being a passenger. As the driver I have to be completely focused and in tune with my car, my crew, and my surroundings. Emotions are a distraction. Emotion in a race car is a demon we must expel. That's hard for people to understand, but it's a discipline those of us who drive race cars for a living know all too well.

After digesting that, invariably someone asks, "So, if you don't feel any emotion while driving, what is the most scared you've ever been in your life?" expecting me to recall some vivid moment during a crash. They're shocked when I tell them that my most frightening memory dates back to the seventh grade when I found myself playing sports for the first time; fullback on the field hockey team at Andrews School for Girls. When the opposing team charged downfield toward me, I felt the most intense wave of panic I've ever experienced. Nothing since that day has come close.

I got over it. I stood my ground that afternoon, and eventually became captain of the field hockey team. But the life lesson I learned from that experience at an impressionable young age has stuck with me and carried me through more than a quarter century of racing. By confronting my fears, by competing and staying in the game, I gained immeasurable confidence that I've carried with me ever since.

I was lucky in that regard. Because I attended a private all-girls school, I had the opportunity to play sports in the days when little girls were supposed to take home economics and go to cheerleading practice after school. Years before the Equal Rights Amendment Act/Title IX was passed in Congress, I learned to be a competitor, to confront my insecurities, focus

8/

on the task at hand, and commit to doing my best regardless of the outcome. Those lessons aren't unique to the playing field or the racetrack. They apply to the boardroom, the classroom, and life. Girls who play sports are three times less likely to get pregnant in their teenage years, 80 percent more likely to leave men who abuse them, and 50 percent more likely to go to college than girls who don't. I was fortunate. And I've never forgotten it.

That story usually surprises people. After a few moments, someone always asks the inevitable "Are drivers really athletes?" question. That question is always based on a few flawed assumptions. People think, "It's driving a car, for goodness sake; how tough can it be?" whereas others stick with the old adage, "All it takes is a heavy foot and a loose screw between the ears."

When answering that question I always try to give my audience an experience they can relate to. Since you're not likely to have a Nomex race suit handy, wear a lined warm-up suit with any old helmet on your head. Sit on a stationary bicycle pedaling at a pace that keeps your heart rate at 85 percent of it's maximum. Now hold two five-pound weights straight out in front of you with your arms extended and your hands no more than six inches apart and turn them up and down as if you were turning the steering wheel right and left. Imagine that while you're pedaling away on your stationary bike you're also being beaten by a hundred or so ball-pin hammers, pounding away on your back, your legs, your torso, your shoulders, and your head like little pistons. But that's not all. You can't close your eyes or sing a song to yourself while you're doing all this work. Your eyes are focused straight ahead, and your brain is processing thousands of bits of information. You can't put the weights down. You can't glance away for a second. And you can't slow down. You keep pedaling, keep breathing, keep holding those weights out, while ignoring the pounding you're taking from the hammers. Now imagine doing that for over three consecutive hours.

While we're driving, our bodies also dehydrate; how much depends on the outside temperature. The only liquid we get to drink is what we carry in the cockpit and suck through a tube inserted into our helmets. It's not very easy to do, so I usually take a swig while running laps behind the pace car. Also, we don't have time-outs, change sides, or walk to the next hole, so don't tell me we're not athletes.

I don't blame the people who ask these questions. In fact, I welcome them. If the analogies I make or the stories I tell shed a little light on our sport, I've accomplished at least a part of my mission. The second part when answering questions about racing is to leave my audience with lessons they can apply to their own lives.

After years of hearing the same questions over and over again, I've realized that at the core of every question lies another unspoken issue, a nagging thought that everyone wants answered but no one is willing to ask. Almost everyone I meet wants to know one thing: Could they really do this? Could they actually drive a race car?

For most people, the answer is yes. With the proper training, anyone who is fit and who has great reflexes, good eye-hand coordination, and the ability to concentrate can crawl into the cockpit of a race car and turn a few laps. Some amateurs who attend driving schools actually reach speeds in excess of 100 mph, a good pace for someone who doesn't drive race cars for a living. But the difference between amateurs turning a few laps at the Richard Petty Driving Experience and professionals suiting up and strapping themselves into Indy cars is like the difference between fantasy baseball camp and the World Series.

At a certain level, race car driving is a precise athletic endeavor that requires talent, skill, experience, discipline, stamina, and more focus than you could possibly imagine.

Life is a little like that as well. We all have skills and talents, and there are times when applying those skills requires our complete focus, our total commitment, and all the discipline we can muster.

I've found a lot of the attributes and behaviors required for success in racing are applicable to other careers and other endeavors. Much of what we do to be successful in racing can be applied to being successful in life. Indy car drivers just go faster.

I hope this book does for you, the reader, what I've tried to do for my audiences during my speeches. I tell my story of racing and, I hope, give you some nuggets of wisdom and experience that you can apply to your own life. I've tried to accomplish this through a literary prism where I've relayed the story of my experiences at the 2000 Indianapolis 500 and, in alternate chapters, provided a little history, a bit of back-ground, and a life lesson or two. Most of the lessons are woven into the story, but if you miss a particular point or two, I've summarized the most important messages in small vignettes called "Pit Stops." I hope you find the format interesting and the story compelling. I certainly did as I was living it.

This was the ride of my life. I hope it will be the starting line for yours and that we can meet in victory circle!

(End of Introduction)

Pinto in the lake, 1974 Palm Beach International Raceway.
Photo: Property of Lyn St. James

CHAPTER ONE

chpt. 1 > goes fm pg. 13 to 28 = (16 pgs)

DRIVE THE COURSE
YOU'RE GIVEN

Unlike racing, life isn't run on a predetermined course, and you aren't given a map of all the bumps and turns along the way. My life certainly didn't follow any predestined track. I can't remember a time when I developed any grand strategy to become a race car driver. Neither of my parents worked in racing, and aside from the occasional teenage drag race, we had no racing history or culture. We were a working-class family (my father worked in a family-owned sheet metal business) in the small Cleveland suburb of Willoughby, Ohio, and I, like millions of other little girls, was a child of the baby boom.

As young Evelyn Cornwall growing up in the '50s and '60s in Middle America, I never lay awake at night dreaming of one day revving my engine and racing my way around the Indianapolis Motor Speedway. I was far too shy to consider such things, and even if I'd had those kinds of dreams, sharing them with anyone would have been laugh-out-loud embarrassing. Women didn't drive race cars. Women didn't even set foot inside the garages, at least not at Indy. Gasoline Alley was for men only. Women weren't even allowed inside the garage compound. That rule raised a few eyebrows in the early '50s when a wealthy woman named Bessie Lee Paoli fielded a car in the 500-mile race and became the first team owner in history to be forced to watch her car from the grandstands. Actress Barbara Stanwyck of *The Big Valley* fame also elevated the acrimony when she appeared in the movie *To Please a Lady* with Clark Gable. In the film, Gable, an Indy car driver, is seen chatting with Stanwyck in the garage area. This sent racing traditionalists into a tizzy. Movie or not, women, including Dame Barbara Stanwyck, weren't allowed in Gasoline Alley, period. Officials at the Speedway later admitted that Stanwyck hadn't actually been in the restricted area. The film's director had cut a hole in the fence to create the illusion of Stanwyck in the garage compound when, in fact, her feet never crossed the neutral zone. For many years I never thought mine would, either.

Mom loved to drive, and she would spend hours telling me how a car talks to you; gives you warnings and signals when things aren't right and gives you positive feedback when things are running well. She taught me to drive in the summer of my fifteenth year, but she taught me more than the rudimentary mechanics of driving; she taught me how to listen to a car and how to identify the sounds and smells it gives you. Mom was also stricken with polio when she was young, so she had to take a car everywhere she went, and once I was old enough to drive, she let me chauffeur her around Willoughby.

When I was seventeen, we set out for Indianapolis to watch the Indy 500 with a guy named Dave Froman and several of his buddies from the local Amoco station. Mom was a frequent customer of the station, and I had worked there part-time growing up, but the trip was more of a guy thing. Mom went along as a chaperone so I could go to the race with the guys.

It was the Saturday before Memorial Day, 1966, and we got into town early. A trip to Indianapolis was a big deal, especially for a wide-eyed seventeen-year-old girl who didn't make friends easily. When we pulled onto Sixteenth Street and approached the Speedway, I got my first taste of the largest spectator-sporting event in the world, and I was both thrilled and a little frightened. If you've never seen 400,000 people migrating to one location at one time, it's a sight you'll never forget. Hordes of people as far as I could see lined the streets, slowly funneling their way through the track gates. Hippies, commonplace in California in the '60s but a rarer sight than Halley's Comet in Willoughby, camped out on the curbs and carried their coolers and bedrolls into the infield while Ma and Pa Midwesterner stared and shook their heads in disgust. I felt like the whole world was awakening before my eyes.

Mom stayed in one of the small houses adjacent to the track while I ventured to the track with my friends. Saturday morning was the drivers' meeting, a final gathering of the drivers before Sunday's big race, and the guys and I crowded the fences to catch a glimpse of those brave souls who would take the green flag. I was surprised by how small Mario Andretti looked in person, and I hoped to get a little closer so I could take full measure of his stature. But I was a girl, so I was forced to stay outside the fences at Gasoline Alley, even though my buddies had garage passes. They were able to get A. J. Foyt's autograph while I was forced to hang around outside, peering into this kingdom I couldn't visit. Only one driver, Mel Kenyon, came over to the fence to give me his autograph. Mel was a kind man who had been badly burned in an accident. I found myself staring at my shoes rather than looking at his disfigured facial features, a fact that disappointed me later in life. This man had been kind enough to trek out to the perimeter to give me his autograph, and I found it hard to look him in the eyes. It was a moment I would remember for a long time.

On Sunday, race day, we took our seats in the stands at Turn One, and I had a feeling of electricity like I'd never felt before, a rush of nerves and senses that would stick with me throughout the rest of my adolescence and well into adulthood. This was cool. When the drivers started their engines, the rumble rattled my entire being. This race, in this place, was the greatest spectacle I had ever seen. Even though I didn't set the goal of driving at Indy until years later, the dream crept into my noggin for the first time that day.

I also got my first taste of the hazards of auto racing.

Moments after the green flag fell, Billy Foster's car spun out and hit the outside wall of Turn One less than 100 yards from where I was sitting. A. J. Foyt then plowed into Billy's car, and nine other cars followed. Wheels and suspension parts flew through the air like leaves in a storm, and I found myself dodging and wincing, even though nothing came close to hitting me. A. J. scrambled out of his car and climbed the high-wheel fence directly in front of me, and other drivers did their best to get out of smoldering vehicles and run toward the infield. In those days race cars burned gasoline instead of the methanol we burn today, and with 75-gallon fuel cells, they were as flammable as tanker trucks. Drivers who could get out of their cars after a crash always did so as quickly as possible, and all eleven drivers in that crash scurried out of harm's way. I think I heard someone say something like, "Oh my God," during the ordeal, but I was too consumed with the drama on the track to pay much attention. This was Indy racing, and I was in love.

The first auto race I ever entered came later that same year at a drag strip in Elizabethtown, Indiana. I entered on a dare after being teased by some friends. Even though I won a trophy, my mother was not pleased. She informed me in no uncertain terms that I had made a tragic error, and that I would never do anything like that again. Ladies didn't race cars. Ladies wore dresses and makeup and played piano. I'd taken piano lessons for thirteen years and attended the St. Louis Institute of Music after getting a business degree from the Andrews School for Girls in Ohio. That was to be my career path. I would become a secretary and a piano teacher, a nice, sophisticated, ladylike profession that I would dutifully pursue until marriage, at which time I would devote myself to being a housewife and mother. Boy, did that plan fall apart!

After working as a secretary at U.S. Steel in Cleveland and teaching piano part time, I got married at the ripe old age of twenty-three to a man named John Carusso. Even though I taught piano on the side, my family was far from wealthy and I had to work to support myself. John had started an electronics business in Ft. Lauderdale, Florida, a spot as exotic to me as Tahiti. Anything south of Cleveland was a tropical paradise as far as I was concerned, and the thought of living in South Florida gave me goose bumps. Throw in the fact that I would be helping John run his business—that my husband and I would be partners and live together in paradise!—and it seemed too good to be true. Still, I was young and shy and unsure of myself. It took me a couple of months to agree to move.

John also reintroduced me to racing (our second date was another trip to the Indy 500), and he put me behind the wheel of a race car for the first time. It was 1974. We'd been married four years, and John had been racing for a little more than one of those years. He loved cars, and I loved him and cars, so we bought a 1973 Ford Pinto (a car that was later the center of controversy because of several rear impact explosions) and modified it, adding a roll bar, a five-point seat belt, and a fire extinguisher, so John could go to race school. I always thought that Pinto was a great car, and John enjoyed running in the

local Sports Car Club of America (SCCA) races in West Palm
Beach, Lakeland, Daytona, and Sebring, Florida. The Pinto
also was my street car.

I was the gofer girl on John's crew, running errands, making sandwiches, and lending a hand in the garage when
needed. The other mechanics were somewhat dismayed by my
interest in the technical aspects of the car, and they were surprised by my willingness to jump in and get my hands dirty.
Sports car racing had progressed a little on the gender-equal-
ity front by that time, but the sport was still light-years behind
the rest of the world.

In early 1974 John moved up to the B Production class in
the Florida Region SCCA, driving his Corvette in a much
faster, more competitive league than the Pinto-driving crowd.
After a great deal of pestering and nagging, John finally agreed
that I could give racing a try. We had the car anyway; it was
ready to race; and I certainly wanted to be a racer, even if it
was only at the amateur level. With John's help, I enrolled in
the two driving schools SCCA requires before you are allowed
to race. I was twenty-seven years old, but the day I strapped
myself into that car on a racetrack I felt like I had been reborn.
I was alive! This was the feeling I had always wanted out of
life.

SCCA driving schools aren't akin to fighter jet training,
but they are pretty comprehensive. Local chapters host these
schools at tracks all over the country, and the instructors are
volunteers who hold national race licenses. Unfortunately, the
quality of the instruction can be hit or miss. Having a national

racing license means you've been racing a long time. It doesn't mean you're any good, and it certainly doesn't qualify you to teach others. Some SCCA instructors are great drivers and excellent teachers. Others come into the schools with good intentions and dubious credentials.

I was lucky. My first instructor would barely look at me. I was a female and had no business in a race car, or so he thought. When I complained to the chief, I was assigned the best instructor the school had to offer, an Italian professional who rode with me in the Pinto, then drove the car while I rode along. He talked to me about the feel of the car, often drawing maps of the track in the South Florida sand to make his points. He was a fantastic teacher, and I soaked up every sylla- ble like a sponge. He also made sure I understood my respon- sibilities as a driver. Racing might appear to be inherently dangerous, but contrary to what some believe, race car drivers don't have a death wish. We are not maverick road warriors. We race hard and run to win, but we do our best to drive safely and responsibly. That was the message my first instruc- tors taught me and it's the message I tell students at my driver development program today. In 1974, I listened to those instructors, and I learned enough to make my racing debut a few months later.

It was at the Palm Beach International Raceway, a popular road track (now called Morosso Motorsport Park) near what is now PGA International Boulevard. Back then it was little more than open fields and a couple of swamps. PBIR, as it was called, was our home track, and John had been racing there long enough to gain veteran status. I knew all the track workers, and I was friendly with most of the crews, but that didn't sway anyone when it came time to plaster the big "X" on my Pinto. All recent race-school graduates had to run four races with the cross on their cars. This let the track staff identify you as a rookie. As if I wasn't anxious enough crawling into a race car for the first time in competition, the "X" ensured that I would be monitored more closely than the veteran drivers. Every mistake would be watched and analyzed, and everyone would leave with an opinion about my skills. If you had learned something in your schools, hopefully it would show up early. If not, the big "X" told everyone that you were a novice.

I was determined not to be one of those drivers who caused track officials to say things like, "Oh, no, there's a woman driver." I had learned a thing or two at race school, and I was going to show the world that I belonged in a race car as much or more than anyone else out there.

The Scuba divers never entered my mind. Like much of South Florida, PBIR was surrounded by canals, small ponds, and murky wetlands where all sorts of reptiles and amphibious creatures dwelled. Before any races could be run, divers had to be stationed around the track. I'd never seen anyone drive a car into the water, so I assumed these Scuba divers were a precautionary measure, maybe dictated by the raceway's insurance carrier or some overzealous attorney who thought the divers might protect the track from litigation. I never saw them standing ready in their wetsuits, so I never gave them a second thought.

Once the race began I ran with quiet confidence and authority. I wasn't going to win—I knew that going in—but I also wasn't screwing up, and that was a major accomplishment. I rounded the turns focused on my lines, just as I had been taught, and I kept my eyes on the track ahead of me. What I didn't do was check my mirrors. That proved to be a terrible mistake.

The leaders lapped me, which meant they gained a complete lap on me, and came up on my rear. I wasn't checking behind me, so I didn't see them. I just watched my lines, and concentrated on making nice smooth entries and exits into each of the turns. This wasn't so bad. In fact, I was doing great!

Suddenly a little Sprite roared around me. It was like someone had jumped out of a dark closet and yelled "Boo!" I jumped and shuddered. Then I lost control.

The rear wheels of the Pinto shot around and I spun the car toward the edge of the track. Asphalt turned to grass, which quickly turned to sand. The car was off the track, still spinning as I fought the wheel and tried to regain control. Then the spinning slowed as though I had landed in a puddle of glue. I looked out and saw that I was in one of those murky wetlands, the kind of hole where vegetation grew out of black water and gooey muck.

I quickly unlatched my seat belts, opened the door, and ran for shore as fast as I could. One of the track workers later said it looked like I had walked on water. Once I was safely on dry land, I took a few deep breaths, unstrapped my helmet, and turned to assess the damage to my Pinto. I hadn't hit anything or anyone, so I assumed the car would be in pretty good shape. I certainly didn't expect it to disappear.

It looked like a scene out of a slapstick comedy. The good guys get out of their car after a harrowing high-speed chase, pat each other on the back, then gaze in disbelief as their car sinks in quicksand or rolls off the end of a pier and bubbles beneath the surface. Only I didn't have a straight man beside me, and as far as I knew, no cameras were rolling and no director stood nearby to yell "cut." This was real. My first race ever, and not only had I spun the car off the track, I had run into a thick, black, South Florida pond, a gator hole as we called them.

The nose of the car tipped downward, and the hood slowly submerged as water filled the various compartments. One last bubble blooped to the surface, and it was gone. I stood at the edge of the water thinking if I could somehow disappear, burrow myself into a hole or get beamed up to the Starship *Enterprise,* there would be no evidence that I had ever raced today. The car had vanished. Now if I could only disappear, this would all be over.

No such luck found me that day. When I turned back I saw one of the corner workers trotting toward me, and I saw the yellow caution flag in the corner where I had spun out. I couldn't escape. Everyone knew I had lost it. Before the day was over, everyone would hear about how the rookie woman had driven her Pinto into a lake.

"Are you okay?" the track worker asked once he got to me.

How was I supposed to answer that? I'd just driven my

street car, my sole means of getting to and from work on Monday morning, into a pond. I was wet, humiliated, shocked, and on the verge of tears. What would John say? What were the track officials who had been monitoring my car saying? How many spectators were laughing at me? What were the other drivers thinking? I'd driven my car into the goddamn water! Was I okay? Of course not!

"Yeah, I'm fine," I said.

"Let's get to the corner station," he said, putting a hand on my shoulder.

The race continued without me while I dutifully shuffled off to the corner station, a small hut with a radio and a crew of workers. Five minutes later I was a memory, a ho-hum comic diversion for the day. Drivers and crews went on racing as if I'd never been there.

"Hey, Lyn," one of the track workers near the radio said. "John's on the radio. He wants to know if you're okay."

There it was again. My self-esteem was in shambles, my confidence a total wreck, and my husband, sitting on the opposite side of the track, wanted to know if I was okay. "Tell him I'm fine," I said.

A second later the track worker chuckled and turned to me again. "Hey, Lyn," he said. "John says to tell you he still loves you."

Hardy-har-har. Let's all have one big belly laugh at Lyn's expense. At that moment I wished I had never gotten out of the Pinto. Sinking to the bottom to the black lagoon with the gators and turtles and bottom fish would have been far better than this.

As if matters needed to get worse, PBIR had races scheduled all day. They weren't about to stop everything to bring a
tow truck in and drag my car out of the muck. The rest of the
day, I stood around the track and watched races while my
Pinto lay at the bottom of a hole. Late in the day as the sun
swelled over Lake Okeechobee and the gnats and no-see-ums
came out for their evening flesh feeding, I stood on the bank
of my pond, wearing shorts and a T-shirt with a beer in my
hand, watching as a tow truck slowly dragged my Pinto from
the depths of the black pit.

A shirtless fan standing next to me said, "Any idea who
was driving that?"

I didn't hesitate. "Nope," I said. "No idea at all."

John and I stayed up all night cleaning and drying the
pitiful specimen as best we could. The seats had to be
removed, and I took a wet vacuum to the interior carpet and
upholstery. John removed the spark plugs and tried cranking
the motor. Water shot from every open hole under the hood,
so much so that it looked like a scene out of a cartoon. I had a
blow dryer out, spraying hot air at 4:00 A.M. on gaskets, seals,
and carburetor parts. When we couldn't get the windshield-
wiper motor to work, John took it inside to the kitchen where
he stuck it in the oven for one hour at 150 degrees, not something you're likely to find in the Ford owner's manual, but a
tactic that worked fine in this case.

By daybreak on Monday we had everything working well
enough for me to drive the car to work as if nothing had happened. But every time I opened the door, the odor reminded
me of my first foray into racing. There weren't enough air

fresheners in South Florida to rid that car of the lingering smell of stagnant water and aquatic vegetation. I would roll down the windows and turn on the fan to circulate a little fresh air through the cockpit only to have dried seaweed blown in my face from the bowels of the fan-motor. I figured my racing days were over.

In addition to the full and complete embarrassment of my aquatic ride, it was also a pretty big financial hit for John and me. We weren't wealthy, and every spare dollar was going into parts and labor to feed our racing habit. This little setback put a strain on an already tight budget. But at least it was only a one-shot deal: I wouldn't be racing anymore, so I couldn't cause any more trouble.

That thought troubled me. As the humiliation subsided and the stench from the Pinto began to dissipate, I couldn't resign myself to quitting. I loved the feel of racing. The sounds, the sweat, the speed, the vibrations, the challenge, and the competition were all things I couldn't just dismiss. I had been laughed at in my first effort on the track—something that would have driven many drivers to hang up their helmets—but I simply couldn't walk away. I didn't know why, but I had to continue racing. It was in my blood.

John helped. "Look, Lyn," he said. "Driving a race car isn't something you wake up one morning and start doing. This is a trained skill. If you want to go into racing, you have to learn your craft. That means accepting the setbacks, learning from them, and moving on to the next race."

Those were the words I needed to hear. Six weeks later, I

was back in the car, and I continued to race the rest of the season. Four races after my little trip to the pond in Palm Beach,
I got the "X" taken off my Pinto and I ran with the rest of the
SCCA veterans. I won some races that first season, I got to
race, so that was what counted.

At year's end John and I attended the Florida Region
SCCA annual awards banquet. Neither of us expected to win
anything, but it was fun just being there. As the evening progressed and the awards for Rookie of the Year and Driver of
the Year in each class were given out, my mind started to wander. It wasn't until the chapter president called out my name
that I realized I was being given an award. Unsure of what was
happening, I walked to the front of the room where I was
given the Alligator Award, a newly created prize for any driver
who drives his or her car into a lake and lives to race another
day. The trophy had a small alligator, mouth open and head
reared, perched on the base with my name engraved on a
plaque beneath it.

I laughed with everyone else at the presentation. It had
been months since I ran that Pinto into the water, and I had
successfully put the episode behind me and moved on.

Today I look back and remember what a turning point
that first race was. Nothing tests your desire like a healthy dose
of humiliation. But I drove the course life gave me, and things
worked out pretty well.

PIT STOP

There are no Yellow Brick Roads in life. Every journey has bumps, roadblocks, interruptions, and breakdowns. Overcoming those rough patches is part of what makes the journey of life so interesting. You need to be as passionate about the journey as you are about achieving your goals. If you're focused you'll wind your way along the road you're given and ultimately reach your personal finish line.

CHAPTER TWO

chpt.2 > goes from pg.29 to 44 = 16 pgs

MAKING IT HAPPEN

If you're around Indy racing for any length of time, you will hear one question over and over again. It has nothing to do with cars or driving, but it's probably the one question most frequently posed to Indy car drivers. The question is: "Do you have a deal yet?" It can be asked in passing with an oh-by-the-way sort of casualness as drivers, owners, crew chiefs, mechanics, and media types mill around the paddocks or wander through the garage, or you might hear it asked over a beer at the local watering hole. It can be phrased several ways: "Has your deal come together yet?" or "How are you coming with your deal?" or even "Have you inked a deal yet?" No matter how it's asked, the question is usually answered with a smile and a nod, or with the driver dropping his head and saying something like, "No, I've got a few things working, but nothing has come together yet," or "I don't have it nailed down yet," or "We've got a few kinks to work out yet." There's always a "yet" in both the question and the answer, because race car drivers are notorious optimists. Moments before the green flag falls on race day you'll see drivers trying to "pull together a deal," making calls, meeting, greeting, and doing whatever they can to pull a rabbit out of a hat in the few fleeting moments they have left.

The "deal" they are all searching for is sponsorship, a partnership of sorts where an individual or entity provides the driver with enough cash to go racing. This cash might come from a wealthy philanthropist who loves racing and wants to see his name emblazoned on a race car, or from a foundation, corporation, or franchise. But most of the money in racing comes from major corporations, large companies with big marketing budgets and at least one senior executive who sees the value in sponsoring a car, driver, or team. These corporate partnerships can bring in up to 90 percent of the revenues to racing teams. They drive the sport. One of the frequent criticisms of racing is that the cars are nothing more than motorized billboards, but those decals, no matter how gaudy, are what keep our wheels turning. And it is the drivers, those of us who spend our lives yearning to get behind the wheel of a race car, who become the brokers, pounding the pavement, making sales calls, attending meetings, and shouldering most of the burden of marrying corporate sponsors with the teams.

It's an oddity of motor racing that drivers are the point people in securing sponsorships. In team sports like basket-

In the cockpit of 2000 Yellow Freight Race Car: Nomex driver's suit,
gloves; Kevlar helmet; drinking tube.
Photo: Courtesy of William J. Ray/Photos by Ray

ball and football, an athlete signs a contract for a salary, maybe a signing bonus, and various lucrative perks. If the player has a good agent, he or she might then sign contracts to endorse sneakers, soft drinks, underwear, or soap.

Racing is a little different. Unlike other professional team sports, race car drivers aren't drafted or recruited, and there are no pension funds, stock options, or salary caps. Race car drivers make their own way. A driver normally secures a ride by going out in the open market and finding a corporate sponsor who wants to be in racing. Then the driver approaches a team owner with a "deal," which means the driver has, on his or her own, brought some funding to the table. For the team owner to say, "Welcome aboard," the check has to be substantial enough to cover some of the expenses of running a car, as well as pay for the driver's salary. Total expenses can range anywhere from $500,000 for a one-race deal, to $10 million for a season.

This is an expensive sport, and one of the few where the driver—the team quarterback, if you will—is expected to bring his or her own salary to the negotiating table. Can you imagine if the Chicago Bulls had said to Jordan, "Michael, we'd love to have you play here, but how much money can you get Nike to pay us to sign you?"

As odd as it seems, that's exactly the way racing deals are structured. Drivers sell themselves to the outside world, then try to find an owner who will hire them for the money they can bring to the team. With that money, team owners pay a crew, run the race, and entertain hundreds of VIPs throughout the event. The corporation gets its name and logo displayed on the car, race suits, hats, pit walls, paddocks, and garages, as well as plenty of television and print media exposure, and some nice hospitality during the race. But the driver gets the ultimate prize: a ride.

In my over twenty-five years in racing I have made thousands of phone calls, sent out hundreds of packets, met with countless CEOs and marketing directors, and pitched myself to Fortune 500 companies, presidents of local banks, and everyone in between. In the year 2000, at age fifty-three, the game hadn't changed. I was still making calls, negotiating deals, and earning rides by generating sponsorships. I knew the game, and I played it with the best.

In my early days as a professional I navigated my way into the field at the 12 Hours of Sebring by finding a sponsor who would provide tires for the team. That was an expense the owner didn't have to shell out, so, voila! I had a ride.

Unfortunately, raising sponsorship money isn't as cut-and-dried as driving a race car. At least in racing you know the rules ahead of time. You know when the race is going to start, and you know how many laps you have to run. Barring an accident or some unforeseen event, the fastest car usually wins. In dealing with potential sponsors there are no rules, at least none I've been able to discern in more than two decades of raising money. All I've been able to determine for sure is that all big corporations have marketing budgets, and some of the dollars in those budgets can be set aside for sports marketing, which is a corporate catchphrase that encompasses everything from a multimillion-dollar endorsement deal with a golfer or an NBA star to sponsoring a youth league baseball team. As someone vying for those "sports marketing" dollars, I had to poke and prod my way through organizational charts by making phone calls, setting up meetings, getting shuffled here and there, and sticking my foot in doors that were more than 90 percent closed. I learned that to be a successful race car driver you have to be a creative salesperson, but I figured if that's what it took to get in a race car, I would sell myself to anyone who would listen.

Late in 1999 I wasn't having much luck on the sponsorship front, and I was growing increasingly frustrated. What did I have to do? I'd been the first female Rookie of the Year in Indy 500 history, the oldest rookie in Indy 500 history, and I'd always given my sponsors a bigger return on their investment than just about anyone in racing. After I qualified in the sixth spot in 1994, McDonald's came on board as a sponsor, and video clips of me driving with the Golden Arches on the car were still being shown! I'd been on the *Late Show with David Letterman* and *Good Morning America*. I'd appeared in *Sports Illustrated, People* magazine, *Harper's Bazaar, Time, Elle,* and every newspaper from the *New York Times* to the *San Diego Union-Tribune.* I'd even been to the White House on four separate occasions. How many race car drivers could say that? Yet, nine years after I made my Indy debut, I was still running up against the same roadblocks I'd been encountering for most of my career. I was a woman, which was great in terms of differentiating myself and gaining exposure, but most compa-

(chpt. 2)

nies looking to sponsor auto racing catered to a male audience. Pennzoil, Budweiser, Home Depot, Champion Spark
Plug—none of them could connect with the idea of a woman
Indy car driver. They were catering to men, and a female driver didn't compute. On the other side, companies like Revlon
that catered to a female audience couldn't imagine spending
precious marketing dollars on racing. Women who buy makeup
don't go to the racetrack, or so the thinking went. Why should
companies catering to women sponsor a race car?

I had answers to all those questions, but no one wanted to
listen. JC Penney sponsored my car for three years, and independent media analysts calculated that their exposure was
worth four times what they paid for it. Still, every call I made,
every meeting I attended, every letter and packet I sent out
resulted in the same response: "Sorry, we'd love to, but . . ."
Lifetime, the television network for women, sponsored my car
for three years at Indy as part of a comprehensive plan the
network had to promote interesting women's stories. They
also sponsored the America's Cup all-female team, America 3,
and the Colorado Silver Bullets, the women's baseball team.

I wasn't alone in my troubles; I was in the majority. Motor
sport sponsorships are a precious finite resource. A few new
companies enter the fray every year, but an equal if not greater
number drop out in lieu of other things. So we're all going
after a piece of the same size pie, and unfortunately for those
of us in Indy car racing, NASCAR has put a padlock on the
bakery.

Seventy of the Fortune 500 companies are financially tied

to NASCAR, and rightfully so. It's the fastest-growing spectator sport in the world, and the hottest televised sports property on the market. Marketing analysts estimate that the value
to companies involved in stock car racing ranges from $9 mil-
lion to $1 billion, depending on the prominence of the spon-
sorship. With those kinds of numbers it's no wonder UPS
dropped its Olympic sponsorship and pumped a reported $15
million a year into Dale Jarrett's Ford Taurus.

In February of 2000, long past the time of year when companies have made their marketing commitments for the next
season, I had nothing but a nice brochure and some great
press clippings. Then Barbara Weaver Smith, a consultant from
Indianapolis who was doing some work for the Lyn St. James
Foundation, approached me with an interesting proposition.

"You know," Barbara said, "my sister recently joined Yellow Freight System as a senior executive and I think they
might be interested. Maybe we should give her a call."

There was no "maybe" to it. We needed to call her immediately. I knew that most companies the size of Yellow Freight
had already allocated most of their marketing dollars for
2000, but at this stage, anything was worth a shot. The one
thing I had learned over the years was that the only bad marketing call was the one you didn't make.

My mind started churning as I picked up the phone. Yellow Freight was a perfect fit. They were in the transport
business, getting things from point A to point B as quickly
and efficiently as possible. What better connection could
they find for their business than to sponsor a car in the Indy

500? Fans and customers would see the Yellow Freight logo and the company's distinctive orange coloring on the most high-performance motorized vehicle in the world, and they would think of the Yellow Freight trucks chugging down the interstates as they saw me speeding around the Indianapolis Motor Speedway at 220 mph. It was perfect! There were no gender issues—everybody ships stuff—and the fact that I was a female driver would most likely appeal to the company's management in this age of diversity and inclusion. Before the call went through, I had run the gamut in my mind and I couldn't think of a single negative for Yellow Freight.

Valerie Bonebrake, Barbara's sister, couldn't think of one either. Valerie had come to Yellow Freight from Ryder, along with the new president. They were part of the same management team and were looking to put their stamp on the new company. "Well," I said, "sponsoring an Indy car would certainly separate you from your competition. People would equate Yellow Freight with speed. That's what you want, isn't it?"

Of course it was, but I knew that before I asked the question. Valerie agreed, suggested we set up a meeting, and gave us the phone number of Greg Reid, the person we needed to contact.

Unfortunately, Greg wasn't the easiest person in the world to reach. Numerous calls were placed to Greg's office and messages were left sounding urgent and dropping all the right names, but the calls went unreturned. Finally, when my team owner, Dick Simon, asked me what had happened to the Yellow Freight deal, I decided to find out once and for all. Dick and I went to the Indy Racing League (IRL) office and put in another call to Greg. I dialed the number and heard the familiar voice.

"You've reached the voice mail box for Greg Reid. Please leave a message after the tone."

This time I left a message out of character for me.

"Greg, this is Lyn St. James. It is my understanding that you have some interest in becoming involved with our Indy 500 program. For someone who claims to be interested but hasn't returned the numerous phone calls we've placed, it certainly doesn't say much about how Yellow Freight does business. I'm here in the IRL office with Dick Simon and would appreciate a call back. If you're not interested, fine—call back and say so. But if you are interested, we need to talk as soon as possible."

Dick's jaw dropped. He was as aggressive as any owner in racing, but he wasn't accustomed to being that blunt with sponsors. "Lyn, do you realize what you just said?" he asked. "He'll probably never call now, and if he does, I doubt he'll do a deal."

"Look," I said, trying to soothe Dick's obviously wounded sensibilities, "maybe this will get his attention. It's easy for people to keep moving you to tomorrow's to-do list. Well, it's tomorrow. You know, the squeaky wheel gets the . . ."

The little musical chime I had programmed into my cell phone interrupted me. "Well," I said when I checked the caller-ID, "looks like we're about to get our answer." I pressed the SEND key and said, "Hello, Lyn St. James speaking."

"Hello, Lyn," a cheerful voice said on the other end. "It's Greg Reid. I'm sorry I missed your calls. I've just been swamped here."

"Oh, hi, Greg," I said while giving Dick my best I-told-you-so smile.

Greg was full of apologies. We went into the details about what we could do for Yellow Freight and how critical the timing was, and how important it was to have a meeting to properly lay out the benefits of our program and that we would need an immediate response. Greg scheduled a meeting for Friday, April 14, at Yellow Freight's corporate headquarters in Overland Park, Kansas. After rearranging our schedules—I had to gracefully back out of a Toyota Celebrity Race in Long Beach, California—Dick and I, along with Emmanuel Lupe, a wonderful Frenchman who was the general manager of Dick Simon Racing, flew to Kansas City, then drove for about an hour to Overland Park.

The next morning we made a full-blown presentation with video, audio, budgets, worksheets, glossy photographs, slick magazine reprints, and enough data to fill a hard drive. It was mid-April of 2000, less than four weeks from opening day at Indy. I knew this was probably my last shot. I was fifty-three, and my days as a successful Indy car driver weren't limitless. I knew that if I missed this 500-mile race it would be much harder to launch a comeback in 2001. Yellow Freight was it for me. It was now or never.

The group from Yellow Freight listened attentively throughout our presentation, interrupting often to ask pertinent but positive questions. In the first few minutes, I got a really good feeling from Greg and the group.

"Lyn and Dick, that was quite an impressive presentation," Greg said after we had answered every question and the meeting began to drag. "I think we need to huddle and come up with something that makes sense for Yellow Freight. We'll be back in touch very soon, but let me say again, that was very impressive."

Oh, God, the dreaded "we'll be back in touch" phrase had reared its ugly head again. I had heard that one only a few thousand times in twenty-five-plus years. After the first hundred or so "we'll be back in touches," I began to think that this was the ultimate corporate blowoff, the Wall Street equivalent of "The check is in the mail," or "I'm from the government and I'm here to help you." "We'll be back in touches" rarely ever got back in touch.

"We'd appreciate that," I said, "but we must emphasize the time sensitivity involved here. The month of May is upon us, and this isn't the kind of deal we can just throw together in a couple of days. We want you to get the full benefit of an Indy 500 sponsorship, and, obviously, we want to win the race, which is good for everybody. The only way to do that is to have a commitment early enough to put together an effective program. We need an answer no later than next week."

We didn't go into all the details, because most of it would have been meaningless to these executives. They didn't understand the thousands of variables and hundreds of man-hours that went into assembling a crew, building a car, and lining up engines, tires, transmissions, electronics, and telemetry, not to mention all the prep and setup work that had to be done before I could turn my first practice lap at Indy. By the time the first weekend in May rolled around, it would be a full year since I had been in the seat of an Indy car. If I had any intentions of being competitive—and I wanted to win!—we needed to have a car ready to run on opening day of the track, and I needed to turn my complete attention to race preparation. Every day I spent chasing money was a day I didn't spend in the seat of a race car or in the gym or at the go-kart track running my shifter kart. If I was going to be sharp when practice sessions started, I needed to get off the corporate presentation circuit and get in the seat of a car.

"We understand, Lyn," Greg said. "Let me assure you that we'll be prompt. We won't let this slip through the cracks."

I had heard that one a thousand or so times as well, but I had exhausted my rebuttals. I knew they weren't going to write a check on the spot, but we had hoped to get a more firm commitment from them while we were in the room. Everyone seemed genuinely excited about the prospects of going Indy racing. I had learned to read people in business meetings pretty well over the years, and this was a good one. All I wanted was for someone in authority to say, "Yes, we're in." Instead, I'd gotten "we'll be prompt, won't slip through the cracks, back in touch" corporatespeak, which meant we left Kansas with a glimmer of hope but no check and no firm commitment.

The call from Greg came on Tuesday, April 18. I was home

in Colorado spending a few precious days with my family as we prepared to do college visits with my daughter Lindsay. My cell phone rang and I heard, "Lyn, this is Greg Reid of Yellow Freight. I wanted to call you personally and tell you how excited we are about supporting you at Indy this year. I just got off the phone with Dick and Emmanuel, so everybody's on board."

I was stunned. I don't think I'd ever had a company be so responsive.

Greg added, "Due to the time constraints and the fact that we didn't have this in our budget, I had to get approval from our president, so I also want you to know just how much everyone here at Yellow is behind you. We're going to do everything we can to make this your best race at Indy."

It was like a dream come true. Yellow Freight had been sponsoring a car in the NASCAR Busch Grand National Series for a couple of years, so they knew the business, and they understood the benefits of race sponsorship. Now they were sponsoring me, and I couldn't have been more excited.

I learned from Dick that Yellow Freight committed $350,000, which wasn't enough to put together the program I had hoped, but it was good enough to get us started. The first $250,000 would come immediately. That would allow Dick to buy a car and get to work putting a team together. The remaining $100,000 would come if we qualified for the race. It was a shoestring budget for the Indy 500, but it was enough to get started. We wouldn't have all the spare engines and all the backup systems that some teams might have, but I had raced with less. In 1992, the first year I drove in the 500, JC Penney committed only $250,000 total. A lot of team owners would have turned that deal down, especially with it coming from a rookie. But Dick couldn't have been more supportive. "That's not enough to get us through the race," he had said, "but it will get us through rookie orientation, and if we qualify the car, we can get more sponsorships to carry us through." Now I had $350,000, which would barely eke us through if we didn't get more commitments, but more commitments wouldn't be a problem now that we had the primary sponsorship. Unlike 1992, I was a known quantity by 2000. When word got around that Lyn St. James and Dick Simon had a sponsor, deals ranging from $20,000 to $50,000 would steadily trickle in throughout the month of May.

We were going racing. And I needed to get myself ready for the ride of my life.

End of chpt. 2

44

1981 Ford Motor Company Factory driver with Mustang.
Photo: Courtesy of Ford Motor Company

CHAPTER THREE

Chpt. 37 goes fm pg. 45 to 62 = (18 pgs)

You Never Know
Till You Ask

There's a huge dichotomy between the professional race car driver who dons a race suit and climbs behind the wheel of a race car and the driver who calls potential sponsors and makes sales presentations to corporate boards. You could say they are two different people. The person who straps himself into a race car is a focused, driven athlete who won't take no for an answer and will refuse to be distracted by anything or anyone. There is no time for superfluous nonsense, and he doesn't suffer fools. Responding to the car and to his surroundings is all that matters once this driver folds himself into the cockpit of a race car, and anything or anyone who disrupts that is likely to get his head bitten off. The other race car driver, the pitchman pounding the pavement looking for sponsorships, has to have honey dripping from his mouth even while being rejected for the hundredth time. This person is the happy-go-lucky, never-say-die consummate salesman who is always pitching the next deal, always making call lists, always finding the smallest positive grain in a desert of negativity. For this person, rejection is a way of life, and there are a thousand no's for every yes he hears.

How do both these people inhabit the same body? Simple. One could not exist without the other. For the race car driver, getting into the car is more important than ego or pride. Getting a ride is everything. And drivers will do anything to go racing.

I have always believed that racing is like an addiction. I don't expect anyone who has never driven a race car to understand it completely, but the sky is always bluer, the grass a little greener, and the air a little fresher after you've driven a race car. All your senses are heightened by the experience of racing, and a feeling of euphoria overwhelms you. Like addicts, drivers will do anything to experience that euphoria. In my quarter century as a race car driver I've seen men lose their homes, their families, their jobs, and their furniture, pouring every nickel into racing. The kids might need braces, but the *car* gets a new set of tires. The mortgage is due, but there's a "speed secret" that will add one mile an hour. Those are the thoughts that go through a driver's mind. The feeling is strong enough to make people beg, borrow, and, yes, even steal to get to drive. It's also strong enough to make people who have never sold anything in their lives, people who would rather be tied up and beaten than stand in front of a group and make a presentation, put on suits and dresses and make corporate sales calls all over the country.

I am one of those people, but I've learned to take a disciplined approach. Yet even though I am now retired from Indy car racing, I still find myself scrambling for a paper and pen when I see an advertisement for a company I think could be a potential sponsor. I still scour newspapers and magazines, reading *Advertising Age, Automotive News, USA Today, IEG Report,* and all the motor sports publications, looking for ideas about who to call, who to pitch, who to make an entrée to, who to sell.

I wasn't born a salesperson, but I don't know if there are any natural-born sellers. Some people are more blessed with the gift of gab than others, and I've met plenty of folks in my life who were naturally extroverted, but that doesn't mean they are natural salespeople. I was neither extroverted nor blessed with extraordinary communication skills. We didn't have any classes on selling at Andrews School for Girls in Willoughby, and it wouldn't have mattered if we did. I was so shy I would have certainly failed any classes on salesmanship or public speaking. It wasn't until I got into racing and learned how the game was played that I realized I'd better hone my selling skills if I wanted to drive a race car for a living.

There's an old adage in our sport that says if you want to make a small fortune in racing, you need to start with a big one. The point being that racing requires a huge capital

investment. Sometimes, if you're wildly successful, that investment can be recouped, but 99 percent of the time expenses in
racing far exceed prize money. That's why sponsorships are so
important. Corporations looking to build brand awareness
for their products find race fans to be an enthusiastic and
loyal audience, and those companies who invest in racing get
enormous media exposure for their products. Jeff Gordon's
NASCAR Winston Cup Chevrolet, with its DuPont logo
prominently painted on the hood, is one of the most recog-
nizable images in sports, and DuPont, Pepsi, and the rest of
Gordon's sponsors know it. For those companies, investing in
racing makes a lot of sense. The CEO of DuPont might not
know a connecting rod from a lightning rod, but he knows the
value of having his logo on that No. 24 Chevy, and he under-
stands the competitive market advantage he gains by being
involved in racing.

It took a while for me to learn that same lesson. By the late
1970s and early 1980s my driving aspirations far exceeded my
financial resources. After winning the Alligator Award for driving my Pinto into the lake, I upgraded to a Chevy Cosworth
Vega, not much of an upgrade, but a faster car with a sophisticated Cosworth engine. That's when I realized how expensive
our sport could get. I won a couple of regional SCCA champi-
onships in the Vega before upgrading again to a Corvette, a
faster car and a better racing category, but even more expensive to run than the Vega. When I made the jump to Corvettes,
my husband and I knew we could no longer afford to foot the
bills on our own. I either had to get some sponsors or give up

racing, which meant I had to become a salesperson, some-thing I couldn't have imagined in my wildest dreams.

One of the most valuable lessons I've learned about selling is that your success as a salesperson depends on how badly you want something. If you want to sell real estate because you think it would be a fun way to make a living, but you still want to play with your kids on the weekends and you don't want to make any phone calls after 8:00 P.M., you're not going to be very successful in the business. I wanted to race more than I wanted to eat. If selling myself, my driving abilities, and my team to a sponsor was what it took, that's what I would do.

I started making calls and had some early successes. I can't say it was easy. My first sponsor was a hairdresser in Oakland Park, Florida. The small business owners believed I could draw customers from Ft. Lauderdale into their shop, and I did my best to do just that. I learned that people say yes to people they believe in.

I also went down to my local Goodyear tire dealer and would buy "take offs" (tires that were worn) for $20 each and use them for each race weekend. The total costs of racing weren't completely defrayed, but at least I was able to make the car payment.

In 1976 my husband and I started an auto parts wholesale business selling shock absorbers. Owning an automotive busi-ness gave me access to people in the business, contacts with parts manufacturers, wholesale distributors, and retailers. I also learned a lot about shock absorbers and suspension, which helped me in my racing.

It wasn't long before I realized that even the most success-ful shock absorber business in the state of Florida would never fully fund my racing if I intended to move up in the sport. I had been shocked by the difference in costs between running a Pinto and a Corvette. Anything in the upper echelon of the sport had to be obscenely expensive. At the time I had no idea how much it cost to race NASCAR or CART (the Champi-onship Auto Racing Teams, an open-wheel division that includes such prominent names as Roger Penske), but I fig-ured it had to be in the seven-figure range. Racing parts are very different from auto parts for street cars. They are differ-ent sizes, built to different tolerances, and designed with dif-ferent specifications from the parts you can pick up at the corner Pep Boys. One suspension arm for an Indy car can run over $10,000, and that's one of the cheaper parts. Each engine in the Indy Racing League costs more than $100,000, and you want a minimum of three engines in order to be ready to win Indy. The Indy 500 wasn't in my sights at the time, but I knew that if I intended to advance, I needed to develop bigger, broader, and richer sponsor relationships. To do that I needed to sell myself on a national level.

It didn't take many rejections for me to realize I was approaching my sales calls all wrong. Companies couldn't have cared less about my racing ambitions. They cared about selling their products. This wasn't a government grant I was applying for; this was free enterprise at work. If I expected anybody in the private sector to sponsor my racing I had to show some tangible benefits to the company. I was competing for marketing dollars, which meant I had to convince companies that putting their logo on my race car was better than buying another newspaper ad or putting a two-page spread in the local football program. I had to sell myself as a marketing tool, a vehicle to move product, build brand awareness, and generate positive media exposure for my sponsors.

I enrolled in an advertising class at Broward Community College, and I took out subscriptions to *AdWeek* and *Advertising Age* magazines. I picked up every book and periodical I could find on advertising, marketing, and sales, and became an ad junkie, sometimes watching mindless television programs just to see the commercials. I would make lists of who was doing what and then research the companies to find out how they were faring

It didn't take long for me to find one consistent theme in all marketing: every company in the world is looking for something called "differentiation." I knew what that word meant, but it took a little more digging before I got the full picture of how it applied to my sales efforts on behalf of Lyn St. James, Race Car Driver. What I discovered was that every company is looking for the one thing that separates their products or services from the competition, the one "differentiator" that makes them different. Sometimes the product itself does the trick. Remember the pet rock? But when you're selling soap, paint, or motor oil, the market becomes a little murky. Let's face it, viscosity breakdown doesn't have a lot of sex appeal.

That's when it hit me: I was the perfect differentiator. I

was a woman in a male-dominated sport, so now I could use my gender to my advantage. Women controlled the majority of consumer spending in the country and made up half the population and controlled three-quarters of the money.

I had never been comfortable playing up or playing down my gender. In fact, my standard response to people when they asked me what it was like to be a woman race car driver was, "The car doesn't know if you're a man or a woman." The stopwatch and the track are gender neutral as well. Racing is about performance. If you perform in the car, your gender shouldn't be an issue. But you have to be in the race before you can perform, and if being a woman somehow helped me generate more sponsor support, then so be it. I would do anything to race.

My new strategy was marginally successful. Rather than the rejection coming from the company's receptionist, I usually got to speak to someone in authority, and those conversations were more cordial than before. I extended my rejection time from the first minute of the conversation to at least the ten- or fifteen-minute mark. I even got a few "let us think about it and get back with you" answers, which I viewed as great progress.

The progress I was making on the track also helped. In 1976 and 1977 I was the SCCA Florida Regional Champion, and in 1978 I was runner-up in the SCCA Southeast Division in my class, nothing earth-shattering but steady improvement from the Pinto-in-the-lake days.

Then in 1979 I read an article in *Car and Driver* magazine about Ford Motor Company's strategy to sell the Mercury Capri to women. The company was also making a concerted effort to employ more women, especially in nontraditional positions. I wrote a letter to the three people mentioned in the article. I thought I was a perfect fit for that new strategy. Having a female factory driver would break down the gender barrier and draw women into Ford showrooms around the country, or so I said in my letter.

"If you are serious about drawing women to the Ford brand," I wrote, "wouldn't it be great if you had a female race car driver winning races in a Ford car while displaying the Ford logo? And wouldn't it be wonderful to use that driver's image and personality to promote Ford products?" Then I hit them with the zinger: "I hope you are truly serious in your commitment to bringing women into the fold as Ford customers. If so, I know you will find value in working with me and my race team . . . Sincerely, Lyn St. James."

It was a bold move, but I figured, what the heck? If they said no I would still be right where I was. When I got the letter back from Jim Olson, the public relations manager at Lincoln-Mercury at the time (who happens to be the current vice president of corporate communications at Toyota), saying "thanks, but no thanks," he left the door open with a line that read: "Keep us informed of your progress."

I did just that, contacting people at Ford by phone and by mail on a regular basis, keeping up with different personnel moves inside the company. When I got an offer to go to a Ford dealer convention in Las Vegas, I jumped at it, even though my job at the convention was to stand in a parking lot and grab dealers as they walked by to show them some hot, high-performance Ford vehicles. It was August and the temperature in the Nevada desert peaked at over 100 degrees every day I was there, but I persevered. I was being paid $100 a day to be a product expert for Ford in the sweltering Las Vegas summer heat, and it was frustrating because nobody coming out of the convention center wanted to look at cars. They were on their way to the golf courses, swimming pools, and casinos. I was transparent to most of them.

Some stopped and spoke to be polite. The majority walked by without making eye contact. Still, I did my job. I smiled, and spoke, and did exactly what I'd been hired to do. Little did I know that one person who stopped and spent a few minutes chatting with me was the vice president of public affairs and was charged with heading up the new special vehicle operations division of the company, which would oversee all of Ford's motor sports programs worldwide. Another gentleman who stopped went on to become the president and then chairman of Ford Motor Company. While I felt being in Las Vegas had been an incredible waste of time, I couldn't have been more mistaken.

My persistence and contacts eventually paid off, and Ford finally decided to take a chance with Lyn St. James. They weren't disappointed by the decision. In 1981 I finished fifth in the International Motor Sports Association (IMSA) Kelly American Challenge points standings for the season, and I

kept progressing, moving up to faster cars and more competitive races. By 1984 I was becoming more of a known quantity
at a national level. *Autoweek* magazine named me Rookie of
the Year in the IMSA Grand Touring (GT) division, and in
1985 I was named the IMSA Norelco Driver of the Year. All of
a sudden, I had a name race fans were starting to recognize. I
wasn't a Foyt, Andretti, Allison, or Petty, but I wasn't Lyn
"What's Her Name" anymore, either. In 1986, *McCall's* magazine named me Woman of the Year, and Ford experienced
another PR bonanza. I had enough press clippings and a solid
enough résumé that I felt confident sending out packages to
national companies. In fact, in 1988 I was successful in getting
Procter & Gamble's Secret deodorant brand as a sponsor.

By 1989 I knew I wanted to race Indy cars, but I had a
tough time selling myself as an Indy car racer. I'd only driven
an open-wheel car one time (a story I'll get into later), and
it was tough to convince sponsors to shell out big bucks to
somebody who had never driven a competitive lap in an
Indy car and had never raced on an oval track. The standard
response was, "Let me get this straight; you've never raced at
Indy, you've never raced on an oval, and you've only driven
an Indy car one time. And you want how much money?"

In 1990, after close to 150 rejections, I approached Dick
Simon and asked for his help and advice.

"So, do you think it would help if you turned a few laps at
Indy?" Dick said.

My eyes widened. "You mean the Indianapolis Motor
Speedway?" I said, assuming Dick had made a mistake.

Nobody could just show up and turn a few laps at Indy. Unlike other tracks around the country, you couldn't rent the Speedway for a day. It was hallowed ground, and Tony George and his family intended to keep it that way. You couldn't even jog around the track, a fact I discovered a little after sunrise one morning when I tried to take a little two-and-a-half mile run around the track. A security guard was there in no time to escort me from the premises, saying afterward, "Don't feel bad. They wouldn't even let Roger Penske ride his bicycle around the track." Dick had to be mistaken. I was more likely to pilot the space shuttle than turn a few laps at Indy.

"Sure you can," Dick said. "I've got to do some testing there in a few weeks, and we'll do it then."

"Are you sure, Dick?" I asked. "I mean, I can't see the Speedway management letting me out there, especially if you tell them I've only driven an open-wheel car one time in my life."

Dick just shrugged and gave me that ear-to-ear smile of his. "Hey kiddo, you never know till you ask," he said.

He was right. After two days of negotiations (with me camping out in my friend John Mecom's suite behind Turn Two) Dick pulled it off. I got to turn a few laps at Indy as long as I didn't exceed 180 mph. Since I hadn't been through rookie orientation, the management imposed a speed limit, which I promptly broke, inching up to 187 mph before bringing the car in. Dick had done it. He had gotten me on the Indianapolis Motor Speedway, the equivalent of slipping out to Center Court at Wimbledon to take a tennis lesson, simply by being gutsy enough to ask, and persistent enough not to take no for an answer. It was a lesson I would never forget.

A year later I put that lesson to good use. My dear friend Art Schultz put me in contact with a lady named Sheila Plank, a successful businesswoman in Washington, D.C., and a person Art said would "be someone I think can help you in your pursuit of sponsorships." He was right. Sheila arranged for me to meet Carrie Rozelle, the wife of former NFL commissioner Pete Rozelle. Carrie served on the board of the United Way and was about as connected as you could get, and a race fan to boot.

We met at a WTA tennis tournament in Palos Verdes, California, where we had lunch on the veranda between matches. "I think it's so wonderful that you're breaking all these barriers in racing," Carrie said.

So far so good, I thought. She obviously knew a little bit about my career. "Thanks," I said. "You know, what I really want to do is race in the Indianapolis 500, but I'm having a heck of a time finding sponsors. It's been a dozen years since Janet Guthrie broke the gender barrier at Indy, and we haven't had a single woman in the race since then."

"What do you mean you can't find sponsors?" Carrie asked.

I gave her the five-minute version of my quest for sponsorships, along with the tale of the 150 or so rejections I'd received by that point.

"I just can't believe that," Carrie said. "What are those people thinking? You'd be perfect for any company. No matter how you finished in the race, the mere fact that you're the only woman driver should be enough return on their investment. You'll certainly get plenty of exposure."

"That's what I think," I said. "I just wish I could find a few corporate executives who feel the same way."

Carrie nodded. "I think I can help there," she said. "Let me make a few calls on your behalf and let's see what we can come up with."

Two weeks later, Carrie called and gave me the number for Gail Duff-Bloom, a senior vice president at JC Penney. Within six months I had a sponsorship deal for the 1992 Indy 500. JC Penney and I were going Indy racing.

During our meetings I learned that JC Penney had launched a campaign called "The Spirit of the American Woman" that they hoped to expand nationally.

"Well," I said, "why don't we call the car 'The Spirit of the American Woman'?"

JC Penney couldn't have gotten more for their money if they had bought every commercial minute ABC offered during the telecast of the Indy 500. I finished eleventh in the field of thirty-three and became the first female in history to be named Rookie of the Year. My picture was plastered in newspapers and magazines all over the world with the JC Penney logo and "The Spirit of the American Woman" slogan prominently displayed on the car and on my race suit and helmet. Posters were made, books were written, video clips were used over and over again, all helping JC Penney connect with its target audience by positively associating the retailer with my successes as a driver. Peter Jennings and the staff at *ABC News* even named me as their "Person of the Week."

My selling didn't stop there. In fact, it never stopped. Every year I raced I had to sell myself to new sponsors, making new calls, sending out new packets, and spending more hours in meetings than I did in a race car. Throughout it all, I never forgot what Dick had said that day we talked about turning a few laps at Indy. You never know what can happen till you ask.

In late 1992 I had another opportunity to put that axiom to good use. JC Penney had received almost $3 million in exposure from the 1992 Indy 500 before December, and the end was nowhere in sight. To thank the company for their support and to feel out the prospects for the 1993 season, Sheila Plank and I organized a dinner at the Stonebriar Country Club in Plano, Texas. W. R. Howell, the chairman of the board of JC Penney, along with Tom Hutchens, the company president, and other top executives all attended. It was a fine dinner and everyone seemed to have a good time.

Just as the main course was being cleared I offered up a surprise. I had bought champagne glasses with "Catch the Spirit in '93" engraved on them, and the staff at the country club brought out Cristal champagne for a toast.

"To all our successes, past and future," I said, raising my glass.

They all joined in the toast, which was the perfect entrée for my secondary plan, a scheme I hadn't shared with anyone except Sheila. "So, Mr. Howell," I said. "How would you like to go Indy racing again in 1993? Only this time let's go for a full season. That way we can extend your exposure throughout the year and be really competitive. I mean, no matter how good you are, anything can happen in one race. If we race an entire season, then I can be better prepared to win the Indy 500."

I had put the chairman of JC Penney on the spot in front of his people. If he wanted to wriggle his way out of this testy situation he could easily do so, leaving me twisting in the wind with my nice champagne glass in my hand.

Mr. Howell took another sip of champagne so calmly and slowly that I wondered if I was ever going to be able to exhale the breath I was holding. Then he said, "So, how much do you need?"

I never hesitated. "Two and a half million," I said. That was the low end. I could have easily said $6–7 million, but I knew 2.5 would get us started.

Howell turned to Tom and said, "What do you think, Tom, can we do that?"

Tom shrugged and said, "I guess so."

"Good," Mr. Howell said. "I think we'll go racing next year, Lyn, assuming you're up to it."

"Yes, sir," I said. "I think we're going to have a great year." I believe I demonstrated to W. R. Howell something he already knew about me.

Later that night, Sheila Plank and I said simultaneously, "You never know till you ask."

PIT STOP

I realized early on that the road to success is littered with rejection. If I had given up after all the no's I ever heard, I would have never made it in racing. Sure, rejection hurts, but it also provides you with an opportunity to learn, to improve, and to keep going. After my first dozen or so rejections I finally realized that nothing in my life changed after someone told me no. I realized that "no" was not a personal insult; it was simply a no from that person on that day. Had I been scared of rejection, or if I hadn't accepted being turned down as a natural part of the process, I might never have learned to ask the right questions.

You might get a thousand no's before you hear the first yes. But for certain, "you'll never know until you ask."

Yellow Freight G Force with crew on opening day.
(Clockwise from upper right: Gary Green, Dick Simon,
John Martin, Steve Melson, Trish Moran, Tony.)
Photo: Courtesy of William J. Ray/Photos by Ray

CHAPTER FOUR

Chpt. 4 goes from pg 63 to 86 = (24 pgs)

TEAM SPIRIT

I had never pulled together a successful race program in such a short amount of time as we did in 2000. When the Yellow Freight deal came together we didn't have any choice. Dick and Greg Reid hashed out a sponsorship agreement twenty-four days before opening day at the Indianapolis Motor Speedway. That meant we had to hire a crew—including a car chief, engineer, mechanics, and all the support personnel— and we had to buy and build a car! Stephan Gregoire was racing one of the primary cars for Dick Simon Racing, and Dick had promised another driver, Wim Eyckmans, the second car, assuming Wim was able to put together the sponsorship money he'd been promised. That meant I was carless. We had to buy a car, assemble it from scratch with a team of people who didn't exist yet, and have it ready to be on the track in three weeks. I was no logistical expert, but I couldn't see any conceivable way this was going to work.

"Don't worry, kiddo," Dick said. "I'll get G Force to sell us a car and have it ready on opening day. You get ready to drive. I'll take care of the rest."

I couldn't imagine how Dick was going to pull this one off, but I'd seen him do some remarkable things over the years, and I'd heard about things he'd done that were so miraculous they were almost beyond belief. Dick grew up in Utah as the eldest son of a struggling Mormon family. When he was fifteen years old his mother was diagnosed with multiple sclerosis and his father deserted them, leaving Dick to support the family by working two jobs, at a bakery and a huge ship repair company. He would get to the bakery at 5:00 A.M. to get the rolls and doughnuts ready for the day, then be at school by 7:00. At 3:00 P.M. he'd go to work at the ship repair company until midnight, then get a few hours of sleep before heading to work at the bakery again. He skied on weekends and was the captain of the ski team. He continued that schedule through college at the University of Utah where he had ski scholarships, later joking that he could be the university's only graduate who went all four years without ever reading a book. "Who had time to read?" he'd say. "If I wasn't in class, I was either skiing to keep my scholarship or working to support my family."

After college, Dick continued to work as many jobs as needed to support his ailing mother. He took up skydiving after seeing a group of parachute jumpers at the Alta Airport in Utah, and within a year he had his own parachute jump school.

One night in 1961 Dick and four of his fellow skydivers were hired to jump into the infield at the Salt Lake Motor Speedway as part of the pre-race entertainment. It turned out to be quite a show. Dick's team put flares on their ankles and free-fell for several thousand feet before spreading out and opening their chutes. When they landed in a small formation on the infield, the master of ceremonies was so taken with their show he got on the PA system and said, "Ladies and gentlemen, I think that was one of the greatest exhibitions I've ever seen. These boys are mighty courageous. I think we should change the program a little bit and ask these boys if they'll start us off with a little warm-up race of their own. I'm sure we can find car owners who'll let brave young men like these drive a few laps."

The crowd went wild, and before common sense could prevail and any reasonable objections could be launched, Dick and his skydiving team climbed into four race cars. Nobody asked if they knew how to drive. This was Daredevil Central Station, and Dick was more than willing to put on whatever show the crowd wanted to see. He tore out of the pits and immediately chased down his jumpmates. Just as he was making his move on the last car ahead of him, one of his buddies clipped Dick from behind and he found himself spinning into the wall. Dick hit a concrete barrier, spun, flipped, and rolled the car twice before skidding to a stop.

"I felt awful for the guy who loaned me the car," Dick said,

even though everybody at the track that night, including the
nervous owner and the master of ceremonies, assumed Dick
had been killed in the crash. "I immediately went over and
offered to pay the guy for his car, but he said, 'Don't worry
about it. I'm getting a divorce and my future ex-wife would
have ended up with it anyway.' I couldn't let him do that, so I
paid him twenty-five hundred dollars cash for it."

That $2,500 wreck became Dick's first race car, and he has
been in racing ever since, becoming one of the most respected
drivers in open-wheel history and one of the most revered car
owners ever to qualify for the Indy 500.

Now he was telling me not to worry; that everything
would be okay; that he could put together a team, buy a car,
get it assembled, and have it ready to run on opening day, a
feat that was akin to moving a small mountain overnight.
How could I dispute him? This was a guy who had once won
twenty out of twenty-one races in a row and qualified seven
drivers in one year at the Indy 500. If he said we could move a
mountain, or stretch a day beyond twenty-four hours, or
build a team and an Indy car in less than *three weeks,* I had to
believe him. What choice did I have?

"If you say so, Dick," I said, with more than a hint of skep-
ticism in my voice. "Just tell me when and where you need me,
and I'll be there."

He grinned and patted me on the back. "You worry too
much, kid. We'll get this deal put together in no time."

I sure hoped so, because no time was what we had, and I
needed to get on the phone and call as many prospects as I
could.

One of my first calls was to Dane Miller, CEO of Biomet, a medical manufacturing company in Warsaw, Indiana. We had been friends for half a dozen years, ever since I cold-called him in 1995 about a sponsorship and his secretary put me through by mistake. On that day Dane had been waiting on a call from the FDA about a product approval, and he had given his assistant instructions to put all calls through no matter what. I just happened to be one of those callers. Since that day Biomet has been one of my most loyal sponsors every year I've raced. This year would be no different.

"So, I heard you got a deal for Indy," Dane said.

"Not a moment too soon," I said. "Dick's coordinating things with the car now, but it's going to be tight. Can I count on you again this year?"

Dane laughed. "You know we'll be there for you."

I got another commitment from the local Einstein's Bagels as well. The bagel shop had provided breakfast to my crews since 1997, and they agreed to a similar deal in 2000. A small deal, but breakfast can get the days started right.

More sponsors would come in as the month rolled on. There was a certain jump-on-the-bandwagon effect that took place once potential sponsors saw a car running around the track. I knew from experience that deals would be made from now until race day. The closer we got to qualification, the more frenzied the sponsorship environment would become. Before it was over we would have enough cash to race.

Once I made my sponsor calls, I had to coordinate my

own staff of paid and unpaid volunteers. Things were about to get hectic, and I needed help with everything from media requests to keeping up with my helmet and gloves. For those details I enlisted the help of some dear friends. Deb Turner, an Indianapolis native whom I'd known for years, agreed to help without hesitation as I knew she would. Deb had always been there for me, and I knew I could count on her this time around.

For help with scheduling, logistics, spotters, and such mundane things as making sure I had water in the garage, I called two graduates from my driver development program: Trish Moran and Sara Senske. Trish was a NASA engineer at the Kennedy Space Center, as well as a Legends Car driver in the Florida Racing Series. She had served as a marketing and PR consultant to NASCAR driver Robert Hamm, and was an active member of the Women's Sports Foundation. To say she was overqualified to be my gofer is more than a mild understatement. But like Deb, Trish is a true friend. She would put aside her ego plus take vacation time for the month of May to do whatever it took to make my race program a success.

The same was true for Sara Senske, who was one of the most talented young graduates of my driver development program. Along with Sarah Fisher and Danica Patrick, both of whom are making big-time names for themselves at the top levels of the sport, Sara Senske had the God-given talent it took to make it. She was only twenty years old, but I knew that her star would shine for many years if she stuck it out and continued to hone her craft. Her appearance and attitude wouldn't hurt her, either. A beautiful blonde with penetrating eyes and a smile that looked like it came off the cover of a magazine, Sara would introduce herself by saying, "Hi, I'm Sara, no 'h,' Senske, like Penske, with an 'S.' " During one of the driver development drills where I had all the students stand up and make a speech, Sara brought the house down by saying: "With no disrespect to present company, including our mentor and host this week, I'm going to be the first woman to win the Indianapolis 500. You can write it down."

No disrespect to the precocious goals of youth, but I was the woman racing in Indy this year, which meant I was the female with a chance to win. And I wanted Sara by my side as I made this run.

When I finally reached her by cell phone, Sara sounded like a teenager who'd just been asked to the prom. "You're in?" she said with a touch of glee in her voice.

"I'm in," I said. "Are you in?"

"Woo!" she shouted. "You bet. Just tell me when to be there."

The girl never lacked enthusiasm. And I couldn't have asked for a better support team going into one of the busiest months of my life.

Within twenty-four hours, Dick had a garage lined up, a skeleton crew in place, and a car on the way. "G Force is driving their truck up from Atlanta and parking it outside Steve Melson's garage," he said.

"Melson?" I asked.

"Yeah, I hired him to head up your car. He's a good guy. I'm comfortable with him."

I knew of Steve Melson, but I'd never worked with him at the track. He was a former three-quarter midget driver who had a race shop less than a mile from the track, and he was generally regarded as one of the best machinists in the business. When it came to tooling parts for a race car, Steve was The Man. He was also close. If I threw a rock as hard as I could out the window of my Indianapolis office, I could probably hit Steve in the head. His building and mine shared a parking lot, so I kept in touch with him when I was in town. He always had cars in and out of his shop, and he was a known quantity when it came to managing race cars. My only concern was his experience handling a crew under race conditions. It took a certain type of personality to manage the pressure of Indy and keep all the disparate personalities you have on a team working together toward the same goal. Steve was a good man, and a great mechanic, but I'd never seen him in the pits on qualifying day, and I'd never watched him work under the kinds of outrageous deadlines we would face between now and race day.

After digesting the Melson info, it occurred to me that Dick had said G Force would be parking their semi outside Steve's garage. That was highly unusual, especially this close to opening day. Dallara and G Force always set up shop at the Speedway during May, and they always parked as close to Gasoline Alley as possible. Each company had a vested interest in keeping team owners happy, so they were always available with parts and expert advice. To have the truck committed to one garage a mile off-site was a coup unlike any I'd ever seen. But I was also a little concerned. Why did we need a parts truck outside the garage when we didn't have a car yet?

"We're building the car out of the truck," Dick said.

I paused, waiting for a little more of an explanation. If I'd learned anything about Dick over the years it was that silence was the best way to get him to talk. He couldn't stand the vacuum of silence, and he would rush to fill it with more words. If you could be patient enough to listen, and savvy enough to follow his sometimes scattered ramblings, Dick would always come back around and give you the info you needed.

"Look, it's the only way to do it," he said. "The last thing we want is for the car to be delivered and find out we need different parts or more parts. This way we'll have all the parts right outside the door. I can't think of a better way to get this done in the time we have."

He was right. It was an unusual way of doing things, but these were unusual circumstances. Indy cars didn't arrive like production cars you bought off the lot at a dealership. Every part came separately, almost like a kit car. As anyone who has ever assembled a toy at Christmas can tell you, there's nothing more frustrating than opening all the boxes and bags only to realize some of the parts you need are missing. Dick was eliminating that problem by having a parts truck on standby right outside the garage door. Anything the crew needed should be on that truck, with Melson's machine shop right inside to modify or make whatever specialty items G Force didn't stock.

Having the truck there was the best, and probably the only, way to get the car built quickly and efficiently. The more I thought about it, the more I realized what a wizard Dick had been for getting G Force to agree.

I decided to test his wizardry further by asking a few more personnel questions. "How about a crew?" I asked.

"It's coming together," Dick said. "Wim's deal is looking shakier by the minute, so I've got John Martin and his guys ready to move over to your car if Wim's deal falls through. Plus Richee and the guys on Stephan's car will help out."

I wasn't surprised that Wim Eyckmans's sponsorship deal was unraveling, but I still felt a pang of sympathy for him. Having a sponsor commit, back out, then commit again was an emotional roller coaster, and Wim was probably as frustrated as he'd ever been in life. I knew; I'd been there. I hated to see any driver lose his ride because a sponsor went south at the last minute, but that was part of the sport. If things turned around and Wim was able to race, great. If his deal fell through, it would be a shame, but it would also mean John Martin, one of the most experienced crew chiefs in the business, could move over to my team, and Wim's car would be available as a backup. I would be the biggest beneficiary if Wim officially bowed out, but I found no joy in that fact. My gain would be Wim's loss, and that was a tough pill to swallow.

As for the rest of the crew, I trusted Dick's judgment on the recruiting front. Indy car teams aren't much different from smaller NFL, NBA, or Major League Baseball teams in terms of their organizational structure. Every team has an owner, a general manager, a car chief, and various assistant

73

RIDE OF YOUR LIFE 73

mechanics and engineers. Then you have the support staff, which includes the truck drivers, the PR people, the runners who keep up with the tires and all the pit equipment, as well as the hospitality staff who entertain sponsors and guests throughout the week. Each team also has its fair share of groupie hangers-on, those who maneuver their way into the race scene without contributing very much. A crew can range from five to thirty full-time people depending on the size and scope of the operation. When a team owner races more than one car, the numbers grow proportionally.

In our case we didn't need the entire crew to show up at once, but we did need specialized mechanics to arrive at precise times in the evolutionary process of the car. For example, we didn't need engine and transmission experts around on the days we were building the suspension, and we didn't need engineers hanging around on the days we were adding the plumbing and cooling systems. We didn't need tire guys around on the days we were building the seat, and we didn't need anybody around on the days we were painting the car. What we did need was for all of those people to be ready the instant it came time for their specialty. That was going to take a great deal of logistical coordination. At that moment I was glad it was Dick doing the coordinating and not me.

Late in the evening of Tuesday, May 2, the G Force truck rumbled into the parking lot in front of Melson Automotive. It was an imposing rig, the kind of lumbering 18-wheel giant that sends you scurrying for another lane when it comes up behind you on the interstate. From ground level inside Steve's shop it looked like a black wall had been erected over the doorway. To me, it looked golden. That truck held my future in every drawer and cubbyhole where bolts and rods were stashed away for transport.

"I'm sorry about the mess in here," Steve Melson said when the truck arrived. Just because he had signed on to run my crew didn't mean Steve would give up his machining business for the month. Like most race mechanics in Indianapolis, Steve made the bulk of his living during May, when the center of the racing universe shifted to Indy. May for him was like December for a toy store: the month could either make or break you. When the G Force truck pulled up and started unloading boxes, Steve had to move race tubs from one end of the floor to the other to make room. "It's just been so busy," he said.

"Don't worry about it," I said. "As long as we have room to get this car built, we should be fine."

"Oh, we'll get it built," Steve said, a little too eagerly. "This is going to be your best year ever."

I tried to act as cool and collected as possible, but anxiety was washing over me with every passing minute. The car was in boxes! It looked like somebody's surplus collection. We had ten days—240 hours!—to get it ready to run, a job that normally took at least twice that long. "Let me know what I can do to help," I said to Steve.

"Just be ready to drive on opening day," he said. "We'll have a car for you."

The next morning, Wednesday the third of May, another

car fell from the sky. Dick showed up at the shop early and made it official: as we had suspected, Wim Eyckmans's deal had, indeed, fallen apart, and we had another car. But because Dick has one of the biggest hearts in racing, he refused to commit the car to anyone else until after opening day. He wanted to give Wim at least that long to pull something else together. Not many owners would have done that, especially knowing that he could save a boatload of money by simply turning Wim's car into my car and scrapping the idea of building a new G Force from the ground up. But Dick wasn't like that. He would give Wim every second he could, sacrificing his own financial well-being to give another driver a chance. What we did have, however, was Wim's crew, which included a burly white-haired character named John Martin who stood out in my book as one of the best men in racing.

John was sixty years old, but he had one of those sparkling faces that disguised his age. A big man who stood over six feet tall with a 250-pound frame, John could have been fifty or seventy, and nobody would have questioned it or cared. He had a commanding presence that transcended age. His deep bass voice sounded like it was rumbling up from the depths of a cave every time he opened his mouth, and he was always full of slow-talking expressions that made you smile while cutting right to the point. When one of our data people became overwhelmed by pressure, John summed up the situation by saying, "That boy wouldn't make a good sniper. He gets a little too shaky when the pressure's on. He's like an old oak tree; he needs a lot of curing before going to the barrel."

But it wasn't John's good-ol'-boyisms that endeared him to the crew and made him such an effective leader; it was his history, a history every man and woman who walked through the shop knew. John had raced Indy cars from 1971 to 1982, and he'd competed in five Indy 500s. In his second start at Indy in 1973, John was fifty yards behind Salt Walther when Salt's car spun into the outside wall in Turn One and flipped, catching fire while Salt was trapped inside. John immediately stopped his car, jumped out, and ran to Salt's burning car, turning it over and helping Salt out as rescue teams arrived on the scene. John then ran back to his car, twisting the finger back into place he'd dislocated during the rescue. He finished eighth in that Indy 500, which took place over three days due to rain delays.

Throughout the '70s, John owned race cars, as well as a tire distributorship and a transportation company for race-horses, but he sold those businesses in 1978. Racing was what he knew and what he loved, and the track was where he was destined to stay. "I tried to be normal," he'd say. "But it almost killed me so I had to go back to racing. After doing this for about forty years it's all I know. I don't want to learn another trade at this point."

My heartbeat slowed considerably once I learned John was on my team. He was old school, which meant he would get the job done without any nonsense. If there was a problem, John would tell you about it. He would be neither overly optimistic nor unnecessarily pessimistic. He would simply do the job and get on with it. That was what we needed, and I was thrilled to have him on board.

The only potential problem was the fact that we now had two crew chiefs (three if you counted Dick, who was about as hands-on as any team owner could possibly be). The last thing we needed at this early stage were bruised egos and lingering question marks about who was in charge. I'd known Dick long enough to realize how he would handle the situation. He would do what he always did, let things ride and assume people would gravitate toward their highest and most productive uses. I wasn't so sure. Steve was already wrinkling his brow when John told a mechanic to fetch this or that. Given the intense schedule we had to keep, I knew tempers would be short and there would be a few flare-ups before we turned our first lap. I just hoped our best men didn't clash before we got the car out of the box.

Speaking of the box, that's exactly what the tub came in, a rectangular box that looked like it could have held a refrigerator. The tub, the cylindrical body of the car, was the only thing that came in one piece. Everything else—the wiring, plumbing, engine, transmission, suspension, push rods, steering column, pedals, nose cone, front and rear wings, side pods, and seat—had to be assembled from parts on the G Force truck or manufactured in Steve's machine shop. Most of these processes were beyond my expertise as the driver, and I knew that the last thing the guys needed was for me to hang around asking a thousand distracting questions, so I decided to get out of the garage for a while and prepare myself to race.

I own a 125 shifter go-kart, a small, light go-kart similar to what you see scooting around tracks on Saturday afternoons all over the country, but with a 125 cc motorcycle engine. The wheels are about six inches in diameter, and when I'm sitting in the seat, my butt is about two inches off the ground. But unlike the go-karts you rent at the cheesy fun parks, the shifter has six gears and can reach speeds in excess of 140 mph. The sensation you feel in that seat with nothing around you but open track and a small metal frame is as close as you'll get to open-wheel racing without crawling into an Indy car.

I needed that feeling, especially given the stress I'd been under with the Yellow Freight deal taking shape so late, and Dick scrambling to piece everything together. There was nothing like speed to refocus your energies and remind you why you were doing this in the first place.

I loaded my kart into the back of a pickup truck and drove south on I-65 to the little town of Whiteland, Indiana, a community where the biggest structure is a grain elevator, and the only intersection is marked by a four-way stop. Whiteland is what Norman Rockwell had in mind when he painted Middle America: small, quaint, and totally reliant on corn crops to keep the town alive. Whiteland's busiest commercial enterprise is a go-kart track, the Whiteland Raceway, located about a mile outside town in the middle of a cornfield. That's where I spent the next twelve days, driving my heart out every day.

Running fast felt great, even if it was only a shifter go-kart. The speed, the vibration in my hands, the intensity of picking a line, setting a turn, hitting the apex, and shooting through the exit with the squeal of a fully throttled, high-rpm engine rushing through my ears were things I'd missed and needed.

When I stopped the go-kart and got off the track I was drenched in sweat and tingling with adrenaline. It was a far cry from what I would experience in a little over a week, but it was driving. I was back in the saddle again.

※※※※

The saddle of an Indy car was quite a bit different, though, and on day six of our frenetic assembly project John called me back to the garage to begin fitting the seat. Racing seats for Indy cars aren't standard issue. You can't buy one at the local race shop, and there are no production models. Each seat is custom made to fit the driver and the car into which the driver is being fitted. A local designer named Glenn McDonald builds 90 percent of the seats in Gasoline Alley. But John wanted to build my seat himself, and he wanted to spend a great deal of time with me during that process. Late Monday night we met at Melson's garage and began the long six-hour process of fitting and building an Indy car seat.

Indy car seats are made of an expanded polystyrene compound, similar in appearance to Styrofoam. The polystyrene starts out as little pellets inside a clear plastic bag, which looks like a beanbag chair from the early '70s. A resin is applied to the pellets to make them pliable but still able to hold their shape. When you're sitting in the bag, it feels like clay or thick mud. The seat is movable but manageable. The bag is placed inside the tub, and the driver sits in the bag. Then a vacuum is applied to pull all the air out of the bag, giving the seat a permanent shape that's molded to the driver's body. John applied a quarter-inch of impact foam inside the seat where my spine and shoulder blades would be for added protection.

Building a seat is a long and tedious process. It's not as simple as hopping in, wiggling your rear into a comfortable position, and hopping out. All the crevices have to be filled, and the driver also has to be able to drive the car. You have to be able to depress the pedals, turn the steering wheel, adjust the sway bars, and turn the knobs. These aren't big issues when you're jumping into your Expedition for a quick grocery run, but in a high-performance race car the entire setup of the car must begin with driver comfort and driver safety.

You have to start by determining where the driver needs to be in order to see and have the proper airflow over the helmet. Drivers aren't enclosed behind doors and a windshield in Indy cars. Your head is exposed and your helmet becomes an aerodynamic tool in setting up the car for maximum performance. There is a "sweet spot" where you as a driver feel comfortable with your visual acuity and the crew feels good about the aerodynamics of your head. That's your starting point for building a seat.

The next step is establishing pedal position. I have long legs, short arms, and small feet, so I've always needed a false floor built into the tub so my feet are at the correct angles to reach the pedals. Again that sounds silly if you're talking about a production car. Why wouldn't you just move the seat forward or extend or move the pedals? In an Indy car you don't have room to move the seat anywhere, particularly forward, and you wouldn't extend the pedals, because to do so would change the angle, thus changing the way the pedals depress. You want the pedals to be perfectly positioned so the driver can keep the throttle fully depressed at all times. That means you want the driver to keep his foot flat on the floor. If the throttle, commonly called the gas pedal by nonracers, is too far away, the driver's foot will be at an odd angle, which could lead to cramps. All the pedals, including the dead pedal located just left of the clutch, must be positioned so the driver's feet are never in uncomfortable or awkward positions.

Once the head and pedal positions are established, you have to figure out where the steering wheel should be. This is a huge issue because of the length of time a driver must keep his hands on the wheel. If the position of the wheel were to be off just a fraction of an inch, it would create some real problems after an hour or so in the car. Imagine holding five-pound weights in each hand. As long as you can hold your hands in a neutral position with a bend at the elbows, it's not a problem. But if you have to hold your hands directly out in front of you with your arms extended, you'll eventually have trouble. After a period of time the five-pound weights will feel like 100 pounds. Drivers have to steer the car for 500 miles at speeds in excess of 200 mph. A small error in steering wheel location can become the 100-pound weight that slows the car down.

Finally, you have to make sure the driver's knees are in the right spot and properly protected. Knees are a common problem among Indy car drivers because the knees are slightly bent and directly under the bulkhead inside the car. Consequently they absorb a lot of the impact in a crash. Properly positioning the knees and padding the bulkhead area doesn't eliminate the problem, but it cuts down on the risks of injury and bruises in a crash.

A lot of nondriver engineers don't understand the importance of all those factors. That's why I was lucky to have John building my seat. He spent an inordinate amount of time with me, asking questions, pampering, experimenting, adjusting, and doing whatever it took to make the seat as safe and comfortable as possible. I would think the seat was perfect, but John would say, "Are you sure you don't want a little more support in your shoulder?" at the same time he was pushing his hand underneath my shoulder. "Oh, yeah," I would say. "That feels better." I would have never thought of that addition on my own, and a seat engineer who had never driven a race car wouldn't have, either. Only someone with John's experience could have known what to look for, what to say, and what to do to get things just right in the cockpit.

He also got things just right in the garage. It didn't take long for everyone to realize that even though Steve Melson held the title of crew chief, John was the man. Even Steve realized it, and he was very gracious in allowing John to assume the leadership role. Steve could have huffed, puffed, kicked the door, and made life generally miserable by forcing Dick to make a no-win choice. But Steve did none of that, and I remain thankful to him to this day for the selfless, professional way he handled things.

Finding a team leader, someone who would set the tone in the garage and who could rally the mechanics in a time of need, was critical, and I felt certain that John was the right man for the job. We were working with a short window of time, so our team needed to jell quickly. While racing isn't combat, the military model is the best analogy. Race teams are like platoons, with the team owner as the company commanding officer, the general manager as the executive officer, and the crew chief as the platoon leader. Anyone who has ever served in the military knows that the platoon is the core of all operations, and any dissension or lack of continuity within the ranks of a platoon will undermine the entire company. The most elaborate and expensive operations our military can devise are only as effective as the platoons that implement them. Racing teams must have that same sort of cohesive bond. Without it, no amount of money will put you on top.

If there was any doubt who was in charge after the first four days of car building, the fifth day removed all doubts. One of the mechanics who had been hired sight unseen turned out to be an uncooperative troublemaker. He was a good mechanic from Quebec, but the kind of guy who looked for an argument everywhere he went. We had neither the time nor the resources to put up with an agitator who could bring the team down. The situation came to a head on Saturday morning when, after bitching and moaning about working on Saturday, he put a new bolt onto a new suspension piece without first sending it through the machining process to lubricate it and tap out the threads.

"Don't put that on there without lubing it first," John said.

"It'll gall up when we get out there and we've had it."

"No it won't," he said.

The whole garage froze. It was like one of those old Westerns where the entire bar goes silent when John Wayne walks through the swinging doors. John stood slowly, letting his towering presence be felt before speaking. When the words came they sounded like they'd come from the horn of a freight train. "Don't tell me they won't," he bellowed. "I was doing this before your daddy first smiled at your mother, and I'm not about to let you screw up an entire suspension. If you want to pull that crap, go do it in somebody else's garage."

Eventually that's what he did. Dick let him go a few days later. But it was John who had established himself as the team leader. From that moment on, John Martin was the go-to guy for Dick Simon's No. 90 car driven by Lyn St. James.

By the tenth of May it looked like we would make it for opening day on the thirteenth. Richee Simon and Justin McLean pitched in every night after they finished working on Stephan's car, and Steve kept three employees busy all week doing nothing but building parts. Once all the parts were built and the car had been completely assembled, they had to tear the whole thing down—all the way back to the bare tub—and send it next door to be painted.

John was adamant about following the parts throughout the painting process. He's been around too many paint jobs where the car came back and none of the pieces fit anymore. "It's only got to be off by one forty-thousandth and the cam locks won't come out," he said. "You've got to make sure the paint shop knows where to paint and where to stop. The thickness of the paint can throw your whole setup off." John made sure this car was painted right.

When the car came back from painting and the crew put the wheels and side pods back on, it was as visually arresting as anything I'd ever seen. Yellow Freight's color is actually swamp holly orange, because A. J. Howell, the founder of Yellow Freight, wanted his trucks to be a color motorists could see from a great distance. Color experts at DuPont told A. J. that swamp holly orange was the answer, and the trucks at Yellow were all painted fluorescent orange. I had never paid much attention to how it looked on trucks, but on an Indy car the color and the graphics designed by noted artist Sam Bass were stunning. "Wow," I said.

"Looks good, kiddo," Dick said as he scurried around the nose of the car to check the front wing. "The only thing that'll make it better is when it's coming out of Turn Four at two twenty-five," he said.

"I'm ready when you are." And I was. We'd been working from 8:00 A.M. until midnight for ten straight days. I was ready to go racing.

Last pg. of chpt 4

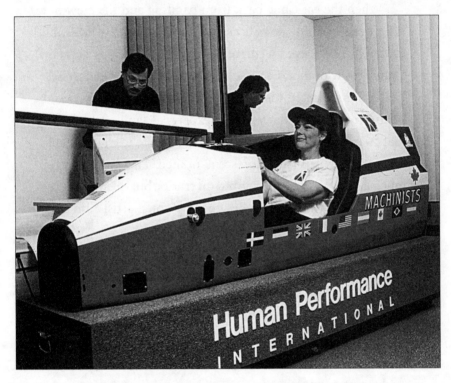

Lyn St. James in training tub in apartment.
Photo: Courtesy of Human Performance International

CHAPTER FIVE

Chpt, 5 - goes fm pg. 87 to 98 -(12 pgs)

THE WILL TO PREPARE TO WIN

The first time I walked into Dick Simon's trailer, one of the first things I noticed was a sign that Richee Simon, Dick's son and team crew chief, had put up. It said, "The Will to Win Is Not as Important as the Will to Prepare to Win." I was surprised to see it there, but pleased because I also have a similar quote engraved on a plaque in my office. In my career I have come to understand the importance of preparation.

In my early days of racing in SCCA and IMSA I noticed that the drivers who won the most races were the ones with the cleanest cars and the ones first in line on the grid. Their work areas at the track were the most organized, as were their crews. Their pit boxes looked like the deck of an aircraft carrier, with everything in its place and every soul on deck standing ready. They always seemed to have the first cars in line during practice, and they always turned in the most practice laps on the track rather than in the pits. There weren't a lot of in-and-out, fit-it-on-the-fly pit stops with these teams. They were better prepared because they had spent more time thinking through the details and making checklists before putting a car on the track.

This was an epiphany for me. It was the first time I fully realized that winning wasn't only about desire, or talent, or guts, or determination; it was about spending ten extra minutes checking the cam locks, or thirty extra minutes organizing and cleaning the pit tools. It was about plodding and planning, going through all the methodical boring details of racing as if every single one of them were crucial to the success of the team. It was about running laps with various fuel levels to test spring rates and shock absorber adjustments as the car lightened; simulating track and weather conditions by adding or deleting tire pressure; and mapping out strategies for each stage of the race before the first car hit the track. These were the things successful teams did. These were the things that separated the wheat from the chaff at the SCCA level, and what separates the winners from the rest of the field in NASCAR and Indy car racing today.

Winners prepare to win. That was a lesson I learned early, and a discipline I carried with me throughout my Indy racing career.

I kept that lesson in mind while visiting Indianapolis in January of 1991. As the newly elected president of the Women's

Sports Foundation, I arrived in Indy a little early to meet and greet city officials and scope out the lay of the land before our annual board meeting, which was going to be held in the city. This was my first extended visit to Indianapolis, and my first trip that had nothing to do with the Indy 500. In the peace and quiet of a non-race week, I was struck by how beautiful and clean the downtown area was. Citizens of Indianapolis had taken great pride in revamping their urban landscape, attracting new businesses and a fair amount of in-town residential development. It wasn't a big city—less than a half million people—but it was just big enough. I'm not sure when the thought first entered my mind, but at some point during that week I said to myself, "You could live here."

At first it was just a whimsical notion, a "gee that would be neat" sort of idea. But the longer I stayed in Indy, the more I realized the idea of moving had merit. John Carusso and I had divorced long ago, so I was single, and there was nothing other than weather and familiarity keeping me in Ft. Lauderdale. Indianapolis was the center of the racing universe. I was trying to break into Indy car racing, so it seemed to make sense for me to relocate to Indianapolis. Plus, all the race shops were there. Even those team owners who lived as far away as Southern California kept a presence in Indianapolis—either a race shop or a residence or both—and most drivers had either a full- or part-time residence in the city. I wasn't an Indy car driver yet, but I was working like crazy to become one, and I figured the best way to become an Indy car driver was to start acting (and living) like an Indy car driver.

That's when I had a serious chat with myself. I'd been pulling my hair out trying to raise sponsorship money to go Indy car racing, but how could I expect anybody to fully commit to my race program if I wasn't willing to fully commit myself? If I was going to drive Indy cars, then I needed to be in Indy. You couldn't partially commit to Indy racing. I had learned years before that preparing to win required more discipline and commitment than winning itself, and I now realized that part of my preparation process was going to have to be physically becoming part of the Indianapolis community.

I made my decision later that month. If I was serious about becoming an Indy car driver, it would help to have an Indianapolis zip code. Within days I had rented an apartment at Canal Overlook, a revitalized area of downtown Indianapolis near the capitol and within walking distance of the Indiana University/Purdue University at Indianapolis campus. Because the city is the state capital, short-term leases are common, and I decided to spend the spring and early summer in town to see what went on in the weeks leading up to and following the 500-mile race. I also wanted to establish myself as a racing presence in the city. This would be my dress rehearsal for a time in the near future when I would be driving in the Indy 500. It was my way of preparing for future success by planning and practicing. If nothing positive came of my move, at least I would know I had given it my best shot.

Shortly after moving into my new place, Paula Oyer, a good friend and fellow Women's Sports Foundation board member, threw a "Welcome to Indy" breakfast for me, and dignitaries from all over the city came to shake my hand. Plenty of town politicos offered to help me in any way they could, and everyone seemed genuinely happy to see me. At that moment I knew the move had been worthwhile. In twenty years of living in Ft. Lauderdale nobody other than the mailman had ever acknowledged my presence. Now I was being heralded as an asset to the city, a welcome addition to the community. I'd been in Indy less than a month and my prep work had already paid off.

A year later, when I finally struck a deal with JC Penney and brought enough money to the table to drive in my first Indy 500, I learned another meaningful lesson on the value of preparation. I'd been to the Indy 500 Festival, met and social-ized with all sorts of business and civic leaders, and become a familiar face around town, but I was still a rookie who had driven an Indy car only twice in my life—not the kind of win-ning preparation I thought I needed. That's when Dick came through, proving once again why he's one of the best in the business.

Days after I put my JC Penney deal together, Dick taught me the practical applications of that slogan Richee had put up in the trailer.

"We've got to go to Texas, kiddo," he said.

"Texas?"

"Yeah, Texas," he said. "The Texas World Speedway in Col-lege Station is a two-mile oval with lots of banking."

I immediately knew where the conversation was heading. Indianapolis Motor Speedway is a two-and-a-half-mile oval with only nine degrees of banking in the turns, the same amount of incline I often put on my treadmill when I want to run slightly uphill. Texas was a little shorter with a lot more banking in the turns, which would make it easier for me to learn to go fast and flat on an oval. We were going to practice to prepare. One of my favorite recording artists, Chris Rea, had a song called "Texas," and I remember singing it after Dick gave me the news. I was about to go to the Lone Star State to get a little more seat time in an Indy car, and I couldn't have been more thrilled.

There were plenty of tracks we could have rented closer to Indy than College Station, but Dick wanted to simulate Speedway conditions as closely as possible. This was more than practice for him; it was preparation, the kind of attention to detail that could be the difference for us at rookie orientation and the last Sunday in May.

When we got to Texas I was as nervous as a kid on the first day of school. Dick had arranged for the same car I would drive at Indy to be trucked out to the track, and we got started around 11:00 A.M., the same time of day we were likely to make our debut at Indy. Before turning my first lap I rode around the track with Dick in his rental car, and he showed me the lines I needed to take and the visual cues I needed to remember. I soaked up every syllable, drawing on Dick's wisdom and experience in order to make this a productive effort.

"Going flat is an unnatural thing," Dick said. "It's especially tough if you've spent most of your career driving on road courses."

I knew he was right. "Going flat," which is racing termi-
nology for keeping the throttle pedal flat on the floor
throughout an entire lap, can be a frightening and unnatural
thing. Coming off a straightaway at over 220 mph your mind
screams for you to lift the throttle as you enter the next turn.
On most high-speed corners, you "lift" when you enter many
turns to make sure the car will turn into the corner. Super
speedways are different, as I had learned during my speed-
record run at Talladega. The long, sweeping turns of a "super
speedway" oval allow drivers to keep the throttle fully
depressed, or "flat." I had never gone flat in an Indy car, but if
I intended to qualify for the 500 I needed to run four laps in a
row without lifting. Texas was my chance to learn that skill.

It took a while. Despite my best efforts to keep my foot on
the floor, I invariably lifted at the last second, a confidence or
"chicken bone" lift as we sometimes called it. Lifting didn't
necessarily mean a driver lacked courage. If a car wasn't set up
properly a driver would be foolish to take it into a turn at full
throttle. But pushing the envelope meant pushing a car to its
outside limits, and in order to do that you needed to reach a
point where you could drive flat-footed.

After a few runs, we brought the car in and made some
aerodynamic adjustments. "You're doing great, kiddo," Dick
said. "I'm going to give you a little more downforce, which will
scrub some speed, but it should allow you to go flat. Once we
get you there, we'll trim it out."

I gave him the thumbs-up. Downforce referred to the aerodynamic forces holding the car on the track, or the amount of

wind rushing over and under the car. Imagine holding your hand out the window of your car as you drive down the road. If you hold your hand perfectly straight, the same amount of wind should rush over your hand as rushes under it. If your hand were an Indy car in that position, we would say you had a "neutral" setup. Now imagine tilting your fingers down slightly so that your fingertips are lower than your wrist. In that position the wind pushes your hand down. We call that "downforce." If you can imagine holding your hand out the window with your fingers tilted upward, your hand would likely fly up as wind moved underneath your palm. You can get a fair number of airplanes off the ground at slower speeds than we run Indy cars, so if the car loses grip the driver can lose control. Too much downforce will give you plenty of grip, but it will drag down the speed as wind forces the chassis downward. The trick in any race is to find the perfect setup that matches maximum control with maximum speed. Today, however, we simply wanted to get my throttle foot on the floor, so Dick set the car with more downforce than normal. We wouldn't go as fast in the beginning, but at least I would gain confidence and feel through the turns.

The strategy worked. As the wind rushed over the front and rear wings of the car, I felt more secure in the amount of grip the car had on the track, and I was able to keep the throttle on the floor through all the turns. The car was a little harder to steer with a high downforce setup—the nose of the car didn't want to turn when I moved the wheel, a typical problem when you have too much rear downforce—but I

(cht. 5)

95

knew we could easily correct that. All I cared about at the moment was going flat.

I kept my eyes on the track, visualizing the entry points I needed to take in each turn and the lines I needed to maintain through the apexes, and I kept my foot on the floor. I was going flat in Texas, and my confidence soared with every lap I turned.

Slowly but surely Dick adjusted the car to increase our speed. We maintained a consistent fuel load throughout, mirroring what we would need during qualifying at Indy.

Finally, he said, "Okay, I think you're ready. We're going out with ten gallons of fuel for four good laps. Give me one warm-up, then take the green."

Indy conditions to a tee. Dick was preparing me for my qualifying run at Indy before I had even passed rookie orientation—a gutsy move on his part, but one I would grow to appreciate as the month of May unfolded. I tore out of the pits and ran four of the best laps of my life. Never once did my foot lift from the floor. My average speed was 219 mph, probably good enough to qualify if this run had counted. It didn't count as far as Indy officials were concerned, but it was the best prep session I could have possibly had. My confidence was at its peak. I knew I could run flat-footed around an oval, which meant I could do what it took to qualify at Indy. Bring on rookie orientation, I thought. I was ready.

"Not bad, kiddo," Dick said afterward. "I think you're ready to go to Indy."

Three weeks later, as I sat in the cockpit waiting to take the track for my first Indy 500 qualifying run, my crew chief, Jerry Cook, walked up and hit me on the helmet.

"Texas," Jerry said, giving me the thumbs-up.

"Texas," I said simultaneously, and I immediately recalled the feelings of confidence I had felt when we left that track in College Station. Moments before I was to qualify for my first Indianapolis 500 an eerie sense of calm came over me.

I'd never been here before, but I felt totally at ease. For the first time in my life I understood why winners in every sport seem so cool and confident. Like them, I had the will to prepare to win, along with some of the nervousness that even the greatest superstars must experience, but there was also a quiet peace that came with knowing I had done all I could do. I was as prepared as I could possibly be for this run. The will to win, it turned out, wasn't what had gotten me here. It was the will to go to Texas, to stay on that track in College Station as long as it took to run flat-footed with confidence that had gotten me here.

When the car ahead of me came off the track and Jerry and the crew pushed my car out into the warm-up lane, I had a sense of calm but focused determination. I had prepared in every way for this moment. Execution seemed only natural. I qualified easily for the field that day. I even managed to place an Indy car chassis in my apartment that was a piece of testing equipment from Human Performance International (HPI), a group of sports biophysical specialists, to practice visualizing a 500-mile race. Two weeks later, I finished eleventh in the race and won Rookie of the Year honors.

And as I stood on stage accepting the Rookie of the Year

award, I knew what it meant to be one of the few. I knew what it meant to prepare to win. Others would sum it up differently, and there were plenty of ways to describe it, but from 1992 forward I had my own personal description for the "it" factor found in all winners. The will to win was important, to be sure, but it was the will to prepare to win that ultimately made the difference.

PIT STOP

In racing, or in any competitive situation, there is no shortage of people who claim they <u>want</u> to win. <u>Wanting</u> to win is like wanting to eat ice cream, there's plenty of it. It's the ones who <u>need</u> to win like they need air to breathe who understand the commitment required to be <u>prepared</u> to win. It's never too late to <u>need</u> to win and then <u>prepare</u> to win.

(End of chpt. 5)

chpt 5

Dick Simon making adjustments while heading out to the pits.
Photo: Courtesy of William J. Ray/Photos by Ray

CHAPTER SIX

Chpt. 6 – goes from 99 to pg 116 (18 pgs)

SEAT TIME

In the state of Indiana, the Indy 500 is more than just a race; it's a cultural tradition that is as old as the automobile itself. Built in 1909, the Speedway held the first race in 1911. Indianapolis has hosted the world's largest spectator sporting event, and for almost a century natives of Indiana have taken their hospitality duties seriously. Hoosiers follow every move at the Speedway from opening day through the final checkered flag, and schoolkids throughout the state can recite race history as if it were a part of a mandatory state curriculum. Average citizens from Franklin to French Lick can tell you who won last year's Indy 500, who held the pole, how many caution flags came out during the race, and what the average lap time was for the winner. It's part of the state's identity, and residents, many of whom don't follow racing any other time of the year, take great pride in their 500-mile race. Indiana natives even give the thirty-one days of May a special moniker, calling it the Month of May, as if the fifth month of the year carried more stature than the other eleven. In Indianapolis you have January, February, March, April, the Month of May, June, July, and so on. It's *their* thirty-one days, the time of year when the sports universe moves to their Midwestern capital city, and all eyes in Indy turn to the Speedway.

In 2000, the Month of May was a little shorter than normal. Rather than the track opening the first weekend of the month, thus giving teams a week of practice before Pole Day (the first day of qualifying) followed by a second week of practice before Bump Day (the final day of qualifying), Speedway officials didn't open the track until May 13, a week later than usual. That meant Pole Day would be Saturday, May 20, and Bump Day would come twenty-four hours later, on Sunday the twenty-first. Teams focus on setting up the car for ultimate speed until the car is qualified. After the car is officially in the field, then the focus changes to preparing it to be the car for the race. This newly compressed schedule gave teams less than seven days to get in their practice laps, find setups they liked, and bring their cars up to speed for qualifying, as well as get a comfortable race setup; a lot to do in a short period of time.

After the chassis came back from the paint shop, we moved out of Melson's garage and into our new home on Gasoline Alley. For all its mystique, the garage area at Indy is fairly utilitarian. Four rows of concrete block buildings are cordoned off by an eight-foot wire fence with exits leading out to pit row, the transporter parking lots, and the infield media area. The individual garages themselves are cream-colored concrete blocks with gray floors (some are black and white), not much different in look or feel from your local Sears Auto Service Center. The difference is where the garages are, and what goes on inside them.

Our new home started out with a little friction as a minor difference of opinion began to fester. It was a philosophical disagreement over how to set up the car. Dick and John Martin had been racing long enough to develop some fairly inflexible ideas on car setups. As Dick would tell anyone willing to listen, "Stiff and low is the way to go." That had become his pet phrase over the years. A stiff setup, with spring rates so rigid they would fit better on an 18-wheeler than your average car, allowed you to feel every bump, and put more control in the hands of the driver. The problem with a stiff setup was grip. Softer springs gave the car more mechanical grip in the turns. That's where the "low" portion of Dick's equation came into play. By setting the ride height of the car lower, Dick believed that aerodynamic downforce offset any grip problems resulting from stiffer springs. He thought ride height and wing angles gave you better grip than a softer setup, and he always made a good case for his argument. "As conditions change, I can always adjust a stiff and low setup," he would say. "A soft setup doesn't give us that option. If conditions change—if we add fuel or any little thing gets out of whack—the car won't like it and there's nothing we can do. I can work with a stiff setup. There's not much I can do with a soft one."

John wasn't as adamant in his opinion on the subject, but he agreed with Dick. "If you'd told us twenty years ago the spring rates we'd be running today, I'd have said, 'Go put that on a train,' " John would say with a chuckle. But he often took a more pragmatic approach to setups.

"Every pound of air in a tire is worth about forty pounds of spring rate," John explained to me in the garage as the two of us watched the springs being added to the car. "You change the air in two tires—front left and rear right—and you can add as much grip as you need. If you up the spring rate and decrease the tire pressure, you haven't changed anything in terms of grip. You've just changed where the car flexes."

I nodded. This was a setup lesson I had learned before, but it was important that John vocalize it again, not just for me but for the mechanics and engineers working with us. It appeared we weren't going with a "stiff and low" setup, at least on opening day, and I wanted everyone in the shop to hear John's explanation. If we went with soft springs, I wanted the crew to understand what John and Dick thought about it, and why.

The soft setup wasn't John's idea. Steve Melson desperately wanted to put a fast car on the track. He was as anxious to prove himself to the rest of the crew chiefs as he was desperate to get a car qualified for the race. But Steve lacked experience at Indy. He wanted to do the right thing, but he wasn't sure what the right thing was.

Enter Tim Wardrop, the Mad Englishman of Indy, and one of the most respected engineers in racing. With long, jet black hair that looked like it came out of a mid-'60s *Rolling Stone* magazine and small rectangular glasses, Tim bore a remarkable resemblance to a young Pete Townshend. He loved the look and cultivated it, often dropping his head and glaring out over the top of his glasses with a brooding smirk reminiscent of The Who's glory days when Pete, John, Roger, and Keith played maximum R&B with a vengeance. I didn't know if Tim had ever picked up a guitar in his life, but he certainly would have fit in at any of the summer rock festivals scheduled later in the year. What I did know was that Tim was Arie Luyendyk's engineer, and Arie was a former Indy 500 winner and holder of the one-lap speed record, having turned a qualifying lap at 237.498 in 1996 in a Tim Wardrop–engineered car. That put Tim on a higher plane than some of the other engineers despite his eccentricities.

Steve Melson and Tim Wardrop were friends. When Tim offered to provide Steve with Arie's setup numbers, it became the Holy Grail. Never mind that it was a soft setup, one of those setups John called "temperamental." I remember John saying, "If you ever find the sweet spot with this setup the car will run great, but if anything changes out there the car won't like it. I don't even think you can put fuel in it without the window moving on you."

John kept his criticisms to himself for the most part. Steve was convinced that we had the secret formula, the code that would break all the mysteries of the Indianapolis Motor

Speedway. All we had to do was follow Tim's advice to the letter, and we would surely have the fastest car on the track. Because Dick and John are the type of managers who want to empower their team members, they decided to go with Steve's faith in Tim's soft setup.

This was as much a clash of cultures as a disagreement on setups. Some of the newer engineers, with high-tech data printouts and telemetry readings, looked at guys like John and Dick as relics from a bygone era. The new guys couldn't understand how or why someone would eyeball the wing angle when telemetry could give you the exact measurements. They couldn't grasp what John could be doing when he bent over and smelled the tires. And when Dick stood behind the wall next to the front straightaway and measured the speed out of Turn Four with an old-fashioned radar gun, the youngsters thought he was nuts. The computer could show you how fast the car was going; the old geezers were simply hanging on to outdated traditions. The same was true with the old-style setups guys like John and Dick believed in, or so they thought. The hip, modern, state-of-the-art engineers used soft setups with plenty of mechanical grip and neutral aerodynamics. Sometimes it took time to dial that setup in, but once you did, a track record might be in your future. As far as they were concerned, the stiff and low setup had gone the way of the 70-gallon gasoline tanks of the 1960s. Today's Indy was about technology and science. Fossils like Dick and John needed to either keep up with the times or defer to a newer generation.

John reserved judgment, frowning occasionally as the softer springs were being installed, but keeping his mouth shut. Had Dick been around, he wouldn't have been so restrained. There was no way Dick would ever have withheld his strong opinions on how to set up one of his cars, but he didn't have time to lodge an objection. He was too busy putting out other fires on opening day.

I didn't make it out for the first hour, or the midday session, and it looked as though I might not make it out at all on opening day. By 5:00 P.M. the itch to drive that race car had almost gotten to me. I wanted to scream, "Come on! Let's get out there!" but I stayed cool, calmly pacing around the garage as John and Steve checked and rechecked the setup, ride heights, and cross-weights one last time before taking the car through tech inspection.

Every car goes through inspection before it goes on the track. Indy officials make sure each car conforms to all measurements and specifications so everyone is operating under a single uniform code within the rules.

I'm sure officials worked as fast as they could that first afternoon to get our car through tech, but it wasn't fast enough for me. I wanted out there. Anything that hindered me from being in the car and on the track was a grating annoyance after 5:00 P.M. I'd waited a year for this moment. Any further delays were unacceptable.

At 5:35, my teammate, Stephan Gregoire, turned the second fastest lap of the day, running 217.036, less than two-tenths of a second slower than the fastest time of the day set by Al Unser, Jr., only twenty-five minutes earlier. The track was giving up some great times. I had to get out there. The busiest practice times were always the first and last hours of the day, with the last hour—5:00 P.M. to 6:00 P.M.—being the busiest by far. That late-afternoon session is called Happy Hour, because it is the time of the day when the cars are happiest on the track due to cooler temperatures, and some of the best speeds are recorded.

Finally, at 5:45, Gary Green, a tall, handsome California go-kart driver with dirty blond hair and a lean physique, attached the starter to the rear of my car, and I heard that old familiar rumble as the engine fired for the first time with me behind the wheel.

"Okay, kiddo," Dick said. He was literally running between my pit and Stephan's. It would be that way all month, and I knew I'd better get used to it. Just watching Dick could be distracting at times. Being around him could be like being trapped inside a pinball machine with bells, whistles, and lights going off all around you. He was a nonstop ball of energy, and suddenly, after spending most of his day on the line with Stephan, that energy was focused on me. "The track's perfect. Let's get out there and do a few laps so we can do a systems check, since this is a brand-new car."

There wasn't enough time to get a lot accomplished, but I was ready to get out there. I gave Dick the thumbs-up and Steve and Gary pushed me out of the pit box and into the warm-up lane. I was driving again!

By the time I exited Turn One and entered the short chute I had worked my way up through four of the six gears. I wanted to get as much done as we could in the precious few minutes we had left. There were systems to be checked and telemetry gauges to be calibrated, and I needed to get a quick

(chpt.6)

107

feel for the car so we could start on Sunday with a good base of information.

When I shot past the start-finish line I was already picking my marks for the entry into Turn One. "Watch your temps," I heard John say over the radio.

"Coming in," I said after turning that third lap.

"Roger that, Lyn, bring it in," John said. "Watch your pit speed." There is a pit lane speed limit of 50 mph, and 80 mph on race day.

After a couple of systems checks, along with some tire measurements with a good old-fashioned low-tech tape measure, I took the car back out for two more laps before the checkered flag ended the first day of practice at 6:00 P.M.

It hadn't been much of a session, but it was seat time. And that was what we needed with qualifying staring us in the face just six days away and counting.

That Saturday night felt like the first time I'd taken a deep, relaxing breath in over a month. I was back in the saddle. No more scrambling for money; no more anxious phone calls hoping for the next deal to come through; no more sitting in the garage wondering if the car would be ready in time; I was driving again, and that changed the focus. Now my world centered on that two-and-a-half-mile oval track off Sixteenth Street in Indy. I was back in my element, and it seemed like the woolly mammoth that had been sitting on my chest for a month had finally taken a hike.

I informally celebrated my newfound relief by going to

dinner with Dick and Dianne Simon, an event that was at the same time familiar and refreshingly new. No matter how often we dined out together I always learned something new about the Simons, and this evening was no different. Before our appetizers arrived, I sensed that Dianne was miffed at Dick about something. After a little probing I soon learned why.

"I still can't believe what he did in the motor home on the way out here," Dianne said.

"What did he do?" I asked.

"He hasn't told you?"

"No."

She cut a perfect "I can't believe you" glance at Dick and said, "We were driving out here from Las Vegas in the motor home"—Dick owned a luxurious motor coach that was the central hub for hospitality throughout most of the Month of May—"and I was trying to get a little sleep on the couch."

From Dianne's tone I knew this was going to be another classic Dick Simon story.

"Well, we're cruising down the road," she said, more animated as the story progressed, "and all of a sudden I open my eyes and Dick's standing in the kitchen making a pot of coffee. I said, 'Who's driving?!' And he just looked at me and said, 'I am, don't worry.' "

"Now, wait a minute—" Dick tried to interrupt.

"He's just standing there making coffee while we're cruising down the road."

"—I had it—"

"Not a soul behind the wheel—"

"—under control the entire time."

She cut another glance his way. "Under control! You were farther away from the steering wheel than I was and I was asleep on the couch."

This was obviously still a sensitive subject in the Simon household.

"Look," Dick said, waving his arms for emphasis. "Every straight road is pitched on both sides so water will run off. If you center a vehicle that size so that the tires straddle the hump in the middle, it'll ride without much help. I wanted a cup of coffee and didn't want to wake her up, so I just centered the thing up on the road, put the cruise control on, and made a pot of coffee. I had my eye on the road. If we had veered off course I would have had time to get it back."

Dianne just shook her head. "I can't believe you," she said. Then she turned to me. "Twenty-five years we've been married and I still can't figure him out."

"Don't try," I said, and laughed. God, I loved these people. It was going to be a great month.

* * *

Sunday was Mother's Day, and I took a call from my daughter Lindsay early that morning before heading to the track. I had married a man named Roger Lessman, a real estate developer and land-speed-record car builder and driver. Roger had lost his first wife to cancer, and he was raising his daughter alone when we met. After we were married, Lindsay Lessman became my reason for being, and I became her mom. In 1993, the year Roger and I were married, I became the first mother to race in the Indy 500, and Mother's Day, which always falls during practice sessions at the Speedway, was marked by Lindsay standing in pit row with a sign that read, "Happy Mother's Day, Mom." Now she was about to graduate from high school in Vail, Colorado, and I had insisted that she stay at home and get ready for graduation. Being in school was more important at that stage in her life than being with me. Hearing her voice on Mother's Day wasn't as good as being with her, but under the circumstances it would have to do. We each had responsibilities and priorities and we supported each other.

We started the session with the same soft setup that we had on Saturday. Our right rear spring rate was 1,300 pounds and our left front spring rate was 2,200. Those are the two most important numbers, because those are the two wheels that absorb most of the loads in a turn. The left front wheel leads you into the turn and the right rear wheel absorbs most of the g-loads when the car hits the apex. If those setups aren't right, you're in real trouble. If a right rear wheel can't sustain the g-forces, the rear of the car will spin around, and you've lost it. You're heading for the wall at that point, and there's nothing you can do about it. We needed to make sure we were comfortable with the setup we had before I put any serious laps together. That was where John stepped in.

"The rear wing is set at zero degrees with an eighth-inch wicker," he said to me over the radio. "On the front you've got three-point-two degrees of wing with a three-sixteenths wicker on the left and a one-eighth wicker on the right."

He might as well have been telling me I was hauling a trailer. The car wouldn't get up to speed with that much downforce, and John and I both knew it. I could tell he wasn't comfortable with the soft springs and the amount of air pressure in the tires. There must have been a fair amount of discussion about it in the garage ahead of time, because we didn't get the car on the track until 3:11 P.M., once the air temperature had reached 85 degrees and the track temp was in the 120-degree range. I got the feeling I was driving a compromise setup, something everybody had finally agreed on before going out. It was a sled, and I knew it. But then, I knew that John knew it, too.

We were dirt slow and plagued with problems most of the day. I'd go out for a lap or two and come in for adjustments. Then it was out again, and back in again. Finally, after tweaking the setup a half dozen times I finally got in a few laps over 200 mph. My eighth lap of the day was clocked at 207.910 mph; my ninth lap was 209.369; and on lap ten of the day I got it up to 209.610. It was a far cry from what we needed, but we were moving in the right direction. John was slowly but surely dialing the car in, adjusting the setup and inching ever closer to that elusive sweet spot we needed.

Just when it looked like things were getting better, they got worse. On the back straightaway I ran over a loose part (turned out to be an air-jack foot from my car) and damaged the left side of the tub. That did it for the day. We were done. Two laps over 209, and we were calling it a day. We left Sunday night ranked thirty-second out of thirty-five cars that had run that day, a pitiful performance. But at least there was a bright side: we had nowhere to go but up.

Monday was another tough day. The track temp was 119 degrees, and the setup wasn't working for me. I felt nothing from the car, no feedback at all. This wasn't going to work. The car has to talk to the driver, and the driver has to communicate those messages to the crew. I was getting nothing from the car, so I had nothing to give back to my team. The only thing I knew for sure was that I hadn't gotten the car out of fourth gear and it was steering like a cattle truck. Then I had an electrical readout problem on my dash. The tachometer shorted out once the car reached 10,000 rpms. Since the rev limiter was at 10,700 rpms and we wanted to get as close to that number as possible without bumping up against it, I needed to know where we stood in terms of rpms. That problem was corrected with a couple of adjustments, and finally, late in the day on Monday, I did post a couple of good speeds. One lap in the late afternoon was 215.414, but I hit the rev limiter in the front straightaway and maxed out at 10,800 rpms. Another late lap got us in at 214.855. We were definitely moving in the right direction.

Everything fell into place on Tuesday. After a great deal of study and discussion, John came out with a formula he felt would work with the soft spring rates we were continuing to run. He adjusted the camber of the tires so that my left front and left rear tires had 1.7 degrees of positive camber, and my right front and right rear tires had 3.6 and 2.5 degrees of negative camber, respectively. Camber is a tilt in the wheels, in this case a tilt to the left. The tops of all four wheels were tilted slightly to the left. For the left-side tires that was called positive camber, and for the right-side wheels it was negative camber because the angles were measured from the chassis. No matter how it was measured, camber helped hold the car steady through the turns by providing better grip.

Why is that important? Well, now imagine tilting your entire body, hands and arms included, slightly to the right, which is exactly the effect gravity has on a chassis as it goes through a turn at over 200 mph. If your imagination worked properly, your tires were flat on the ground at the apex of your body's tilt. Translating that to race cars, camber allows you to have more rubber on the road in the turns when you need it most.

I obviously needed it with the soft springs we were running, and John was just right in the amount of camber and air pressure he added to the tires. My fifth lap of the day I got the car over 217 mph, faster than I had ever gone in that car, and faster than I had driven anything in twelve long, full months. Lap eleven, I crested the 219 mark, posting a speed of 219.973. The car felt great! The changes had been perfect, and we had finally dialed in the setup. By laps thirty-five and thirty-six of the day, 219 mph was my average speed. The final lap of the day was a flat-footed run of 219.521 that felt so sweet it made my molars hurt. This was it. If we could just keep the car like this until qualifying day, we had it made. The average of my best three laps that Tuesday was 219.480. Not only would that qualify for the race, it could put me somewhere near the front of the pack. Granted, qualifying was the average speed of four consecutive laps, not three, and we still had four days before the first qualifying run, but at that moment I liked our chances.

There have been many times in my racing career when I have wished I could shrink-wrap a car in cellophane and unwrap it on race day. Tuesday was one of those days. I knew we had a great car, and if we could only keep from screwing it up between the moment it came off the track that Tuesday night and the Saturday morning of Pole Day qualifying, we would have it made. But we didn't leave it alone. We didn't shrink-wrap it, or even throw a tarp over it for the next four days. We did get lucky on Wednesday. It rained all day and the track was closed. Still, we tinkered with the car, trying to get a few more miles per hour out of it. On Thursday, our efforts backfired.

In the first ten laps on Thursday I knew we had gone backward. The camber angles on the wheels were the same as they had been on Tuesday, but we had adjusted the front and rear wings and added more wicker than we'd had on previous runs. In theory that should have given us more stability in the turns. It didn't, and there were a couple of times when I thought I was going to lose it.

"Come on, guys," I said after one stop. "It feels like the rear end is steering the car. I'm pushing on entry and loose in the exits. I'm not sure what the rear is going to do."

Three clicks to the front wing and 3 gallons of fuel later, the car felt a little better, but nothing like what we had on Tuesday. Seven clicks to the front wing, and one degree more angle on the rear wing, and things stabilized a bit. At least I was able to get in one lap over 216, but the car was still pushing through the apex. We fiddled and fooled around for fifty-eight laps with nothing better than a 216.9 mph lap to show for our efforts. It was maddening. How could we have gone from a car that drove like a dream to such a sled in less than forty-eight hours?

The answer was simple. We worked all day on Thursday using bad data. During our Wednesday rainout, as we were fiddling around with the car in the garage, someone dropped it on the scales, thus screwing up the calibration. We drove all day on Thursday thinking we had a certain weight balance in the car, when our entire system of measurement was off. Once Dick discovered what had happened, he put the car on a new set of scales and we quickly corrected the problem.

Friday was much better, even though we ran only five laps. The car felt smooth again, and I quickly posted a lap of 217.750 before bringing it in and locking it up. We had run enough. The engine and the setup were right where we needed them for a good run on Saturday.

After Friday's session I told reporters, "It feels great to have a car I'm comfortable with going into qualifying. I think we've finally got all the pieces to fall into place at the right time."

If I could have only known what lay ahead, I would have kept my mouth shut.

(End. of chpt 6)

The intense rookie at the 1992 Indy 500. Photo used with permission
of the Indianapolis Motor Speedway Corporation.

CHAPTER SEVEN

chpt. 7 goes from pg. 117 to 134 = (18 pgs.)

FIRST RIDE

I've never considered myself a barrier-breaker, even though I have historically been one of the few women to do what I do and, in recent years, one of the oldest race car drivers to compete at Indy. But I never viewed my racing as a social statement. Even though I'd experienced discrimination and bias, I always took the attitude that my age and gender were irrelevant as long as I was competitive. The motto I've used throughout my career—one that I have repeated hundreds of times at seminars across the country—is that the best way to change things in life is to *learn the rules,* whatever they happen to be; *play by those rules;* and *win by the rules.* Once you've won enough, you can start thinking about changing the rules.

Through the years I've found too many people who want to skip the steps and try to change the rules before earning their stripes. Most of the time that doesn't work. Not only do you lose respect from your peers, you tend to alienate potential allies in the process.

I wasn't the first female to drive in the Indy 500. Janet Guthrie was sixteen years earlier. But some people say I was one of the first female drivers to gain universal acceptance in the garage. I had been doing what it took to succeed every step of the way, playing by the rules, written and unwritten, that were there for me along the way. When I realized I had to change into my driver's suit in the public ladies' room, I didn't make a scene. My team created a private area in our garage, but most of the time I changed in the public ladies' room. My only restriction was that I wouldn't sign autographs in there, or I never would have made it onto the track. It wasn't a big deal, at least not to me. The guys, it turned out, were so impressed by my go-along-and-get-along attitude they spread the word around the garage area that St. James was okay.

I looked at it as playing by the unwritten rules of my sport. I never wanted special treatment because I was a woman. In my view, any special dispensation I was given because of my gender would have backfired and created unnecessary resentment. I didn't want that. I also didn't want any of my future victories to be cheapened by the impression that I had somehow gotten a free ride because of my gender. If the rules were changed because of me, someone would say, "See, things are easier for the girl." I did everything in my power to keep such comments from being uttered, knowing that if I competed long enough and hard enough under the same rules as everyone else, someday I would be in a position to change the rules without turning the racing world on its ear.

⋯⋯

Playing by the rules doesn't mean things are going to be easy. I encountered plenty of obstacles as a woman in racing, but I figured everyone faces hurdles in life. White men, black men, Asian women, short people, tall people, young people, and senior citizens are all met by barriers when working toward a goal. A woman in her forties breaking into Indy car racing was bound to have to navigate through roadblocks along the way—I knew that—but rather than bang my head against the wall, or create a fuss, or, worse yet, bring some kind of social pressure on team owners and sponsors to let me drive, I did what I'd always done: I mapped out a plan of action and worked the plan through to completion.

I never thought anyone owed me a ride, especially in the earlier days when I'd never driven an Indy car. But I knew I was capable of making it to the top of the sport. All I needed was a sponsor to provide the funding and a team owner to give me the opportunity. I figured finding the team owner was the first step. Once I had a relationship with a good team owner, we could shake the bushes for sponsorships.

Dick Simon was my first choice. My dear friend John Gorsline first introduced me to Dick and Dianne Simon. John had said, "These people are the best. They're honest, hard-working people, and Dick is a great teacher. He is a driver, so he really believes in his drivers."

We were at a CART race in Long Beach, California, when I told Dick and Dianne how much I wanted to drive an Indy car someday. I was sure they had heard that pitch before. If Dick was like most owners he got hit on at least twice a week by driver wannabes begging for rides. I could only hope he knew enough not to lump me in that category.

I said, "I've driven at Le Mans and Daytona, but I really think my future lies in open-wheel racing. I'd like to test that theory by taking an Indy car out for a few test laps."

Dick stared at me with his head cocked like the RCA dog. He couldn't have stared for more than five or six seconds, but it felt like an eternity. Finally he said, "Sounds like a good idea; maybe we can work together sometime."

At Cleveland and again in Detroit I made a point of speaking to Dick. "Don't forget our ride, now," I would say.

"I haven't forgotten," he would say back.

"I'm serious," I would say.

"We'll see," he'd say in reply.

Weeks became months and months became years, and I slowly let myself believe that it would probably never happen. We saw each other again in the fall of 1988 at Tamiami, the season-ending CART race in Miami, Florida, and we spoke as we always did. He knew where I stood, and I knew he had my phone number. Since our first conversations on the subject of Indy cars, I'd set thirty-one national and international closed-course speed records in a Ford Thunderbird at Talladega, Alabama, becoming the first female driver to exceed 200 mph in a stock car on an oval track. The NASCAR Winston Cup series looked like my best bet for advancing my career, and my relationship with Ford was sure to help on that front. As far as Indy car racing was concerned, the ball was in Dick's court. If he wanted to take a chance on me, I was ready.

Imagine my surprise when my phone rang the morning after Tamiami and I heard what would become a familiar refrain on the other end of the line. "Hi kiddo, it's Dick Simon speaking."

"Hi, Dick, how are you?"

"I'm just great. Hey, are you still interested in driving an Indy car?"

My heart skipped a beat before I answered. "You bet I am," I finally blurted out.

"Good. We're testing tomorrow in Memphis and I have an extra car. Be there in the morning, and we'll put you out for a few laps. Look, I've got to run. I'll see you tomorrow."

"Memphis?" I said, but it was too late. The line was dead and Dick was gone. I didn't even know they had a track in Memphis. Were there any direct flights from Ft. Lauderdale to Memphis? How would I find the track once I got there? What about hotels? My mind was racing faster than the car I was about to drive. An Indy car! Just like that! I'd almost given up on him, but Dick had come through. I would be in Memphis the next morning if I had to hitchhike all night to get there. This was my one and only chance at the ultimate first ride. I wasn't about to blow it.

Memphis turned out to be a fairly accessible city. I flew in on Monday night, got a hotel room, and barely slept a wink. I tossed all night thinking about what was going to happen the following morning. I hadn't been this excited in years.

Because of my birdlike sleep I made it to the track in plenty of time on Tuesday morning. The reason I'd never heard of the track in Memphis was because it was a drag strip with a couple of turns and a backstretch to make it a short road course. The transporters were already there when I arrived, and my heart raced when I got my first glimpse of the car I would drive. It was a Ford Cosworth–powered Lola, the same car Raul Boesel had just driven at Tamiami.

I was the happy victim of logistical circumstance. Dick was on his way back to Indianapolis from Miami, but he had to stop in Memphis to test a rookie driver from Italy named Guido Dacco. Since Miami was the last race of the season, both of Dick's cars were on the truck back to Indy via Memphis. Two cars, one driver, and suddenly I had a ride.

As much as I wanted to keep it together, every ounce of cool left my body as Dick pulled into the parking lot and walked over to where I was standing. "So, Lyn, are you ready to drive an Indy car this morning?"

"As ready as I'll ever be," I said.

We walked over to the pit area where the cars were being prepped. "I want you to meet my son, Richee Simon," Dick said.

I was struck by how different Richee and Dick looked. The younger Mr. Simon had a full head of thick, curly hair, and the lean body of a distance runner. When we shook hands the grip told me that Richee was a strong and confident young man, traits he'd inherited from his dad, even if he didn't get the looks.

Dick continued with the introductions. "And this is Graham Murray," he said, pointing to a rangy Englishman who was leaning over the car.

"Nice to meet you, Graham," I said.

"Good to finally meet you," he said. "I saw you drive once in England."

I was shocked. I'd been to England only once in my life, and that was for only one day of road testing back in 1984. The owners of a new Spice prototype had flown me to Snetterton to test their car before it was shipped to the United States to run in the IMSA Camel GT series. As I recalled, it had been raining that day, but I'd run pretty well. And this guy Graham was there. Funny how things worked out sometimes.

"Graham will be crewing your car today," Dick said.

"Great," I responded.

Graham said, "I've kept track of your career since that test in England, and I think this is the perfect car for you."

That was exactly the kind of positive reinforcement I needed. The guy assigned to my car could have just as easily taken a "how did I get stuck with the girl?" attitude, but Graham had seen me drive and respected me as a driver. It couldn't have been a more perfect fit.

He also turned out to be right about the car: it was perfect for me. Dick spent almost an hour fitting me into the cockpit, but once I was behind the wheel the beauty of the view stunned me. I'd never been in an open-wheel, open-cockpit car before, and I thought it was the greatest thing I'd ever seen in my life. I could actually see the front wheels. I'm not sure if other drivers have had similar experiences, but the fact that I could see the wheels responding to input gave me more control; I felt I was one with the car. When I wanted the car to turn, it turned; when I wanted it to go, it went in a hurry; and when I wanted it to stop, I simply hit the brakes and it came to a halt immediately. This was a race car driver's dream. From the first moment I sat behind the wheel, I was hooked.

"You have to pay close attention to how you work the throttle as you exit the pits," Dick said. "Most crashes from rookie drivers occur in the pits because you get anxious and press the throttle too hard. When the turbo kicks in, you lose control. The next thing you know, you're in the pit wall."

I almost laughed out loud. Surely professional drivers could get a race car out of the pits without crashing. But Dick was methodical and relentless in his explanations. He rolled the car back and forth by hand while I worked the clutch, spending a lot of time describing how the gears worked and how I needed to exit and enter the pits.

Then he turned to Graham. "Give her fifteen gallons and have her run ten laps, then bring her in and put it back up to fifteen gallons," Dick said. Fuel cells on Indy cars then held 40 gallons of methanol, and each gallon weighs about seven pounds. When the car is full of fuel it is 280 pounds heavier than when it's empty, which changes the balance considerably.

The entire car weighs only 1,500 pounds, so adding and sub-tracting 280 pounds of fuel is a big change. Adapting to the handling differences associated with fuel changes was a lesson for another day. Dick wanted me to keep a consistent fuel level and run only ten laps at a time. I didn't lodge any objections. As long as I was driving, I didn't mind if we did it one gallon at a time.

"Okay," Dick said. "I've got a few things to do, so I'm going to leave you here. Have a good run. I'll see you later."

"You mean you're leaving?" I said.

"Yeah, I've got a couple of meetings to go to."

"You trust me to drive your car without you being here?"

Dick chuckled. "Well, if you were going to crack it up, you'd do it whether or not I was standing here, so it doesn't really matter. If I didn't trust you, you wouldn't be in the car. Get some good laps in, and I'll check back a little later."

As he turned to go, I said, "Dick."

"Yeah?"

"Thanks."

"No sweat, kiddo," he said with a grin. "You'll do great."

After Dick left the track, Graham and I reviewed the dash. The dash of an Indy car is a small screen where various lines of data can be displayed. Because the car measures more data than can be displayed on a single screen, the dash has various pages, and with the flip of a switch the driver can change pages on the dash. You can also program the data you want displayed on each page, which is what Graham and I did after Dick left us alone. When you're speeding along at 200 mph, you don't want to spend a lot of time thumbing through various pages on your dash in search of data. Page one needs to have all the critical information like oil temperature, oil pressure, fuel levels, rpms, and speed. Other data like water temperature and lap times can be on pages two or three. If you need to find it you can, but it's not the data you keep directly in front of you.

After programming the dash we checked the position of the boost dial. Drivers also have the ability to change the boost level in a turbocharged engine, and I didn't want to touch that one. We weren't interested in testing my ability to turn the dial during my first run, so Graham simply made sure it was in the correct position. He did the same thing with the brake bias dial. As fuel loads shift and the car's balance changes, drivers have the ability to change the brake bias from front to rear. Since I was running on a consistent fuel load, that dial wasn't going to be used, but Graham wanted to make sure it was on the right setting before we got under way.

"Okay, I think we're ready," Graham said.

Indeed I was. I crawled into the seat, put my helmet on, and waited while Richee and Graham attached the starter and fired the 800 horsepower 2.5-liter turbocharged V-8. I had laughed when Dick told me about crashing into the pit wall, but I kept his warning in mind. I was careful with the throttle. That turned out to be a good move, because when I pushed the throttle the car left the pits in a hurry. Shocked by the sudden acceleration, I tapped the brakes to slow down, and the car stopped instantly. This was the most sensitive piece of machinery I'd ever seen in my life! Unfortunately, my sudden stop caused the engine to stall, and Graham had to pull me back into the pits to restart the car. It was a good thing Dick wasn't around to see that. There aren't many more embarrassing seconds for a driver than the time you sit in a stalled car while the crew comes to fetch you.

After our first little false start, I was careful about which pedals I pushed and which knobs I touched. I started slowly, testing the steering as I entered the turns and getting a feel for how the car handled. It felt like a second skin, responding to my every move as if it were almost reading my mind. For the first few laps I found myself looking at the wheels through my peripheral vision, fascinated by the fact that I could see them turn with every twitch of the steering wheel. As the day progressed I gained confidence. My second set of ten laps was a little faster than my first, and my third set was even faster than my second. Soon I was posting some respectable lap times and getting a feel for the entire experience. Before my fourth set of ten laps was over, I knew I was in love. NASCAR and all the other stock car series I had been considering were out the window. This was where I belonged, and where I would devote all my efforts.

Dick came back shortly after lunch. "Okay, how'd we do?" he said, clapping his hands together and smiling from ear to ear.

"Great," I said.

"We were just getting ready for another run," Graham said. "You got here just in time."

Now the pressure was really on. I'd gotten comfortable in the seat of the car, and the crew had just put another 15 gallons of methanol in the tank, so we were ready. I could show the boss what I'd learned, and give him all the reasons he needed to bring me under his wing and put me in the seat of an Indy car.

"Ready, Lyn?" Graham said.

I gave him the thumbs-up, and seconds later the engine fired again. This time I pressed the throttle, revving the monstrous engine, and let out the clutch with the intention of springing out onto the track. Just as Dick had predicted, I was headed toward a concrete barrier at an alarming speed.

"Ahhh!" I screamed, hitting the brakes as hard and fast as I could. I knew I was into the wall. My first trip out in front of the man I wanted to impress and what did I do? Crash his six-figure race car into the wall. There was no way I could stop. I was simply going too fast.

But I did stop. The brakes worked just as effectively as they had when I stalled at the pit exit during my first set of laps. This time the car stopped so close to the concrete wall I was sure Dick couldn't have slipped the setup sheet—an 8½-by-11-inch piece of paper—between the wall and the nose of the car. I sat there, stunned. Then I glanced into the mirror and saw Dick's trademark waddle as he scurried to the car.

When he reached my side, the smile had grown even bigger. He sat on the wheel and looked into my eyes, then he chuckled. "Okay," he said. "Let's go over this again." And he proceeded to give the same speech about the clutch and the throttle. I nodded and listened, but I really wanted to crawl into a hole. What would Dick think of me now?

I would later learn that he thought I had to be a pretty good driver to stop the car as quickly as I did. "Most drivers would have plowed right into that wall," he would later say. At the time, I was sure he thought I was the worst driver in the world, and I knew he thought he'd made a terrible mistake putting me behind the wheel of his car. All I could do to make it up to him was show him how much I had learned.

When I got out on the track I did just that, running ten solid laps before bringing it in unscathed. Dick might not ever let me sit in one of his cars again, but at least I had shown him something in my final moments of driving his Indy car.

Afterward Dick took the entire crew, including Guido and me, to dinner at a nearby Morrison's Cafeteria where we ate meat loaf and mashed potatoes and laughed so hard our sides hurt.

"Tell 'em the one about the airplane," Richee said to his dad through sporadic fits of laughter.

"Which one?" Dick said.

"You know, how you learned to fly and the trip with the barn."

"Oh, yeah, yeah," Dick said. "Okay, one of the first things I ever did after college was open a parachute jump school where I would give skydiving lessons. Well, one day the pilot didn't show up, and I had two classes full of students waiting to go up. So my partner says, 'We've got to cancel. The pilot's sick.' I wasn't about to cancel. That would mean giving everybody their money back and I didn't want to do that. I said, 'I can fly it. I've watched the pilot enough. I can do it.' "

"Wait a minute," I said over the laughter at the table. "You mean you'd never had a flying lesson and you took up a bunch of students?"

"No," he said. "I practiced a couple of times first."

More laughter.

"No, no, I did," he said. "I ran it down the runway without getting it off the ground one time; then I took another run and got it off the ground a little bit before setting it back down. The third time down, I took off."

"And you'd never flown before?" I asked in stunned disbelief.

"No, but I'd watched the pilot enough. I'd seen how he handled it."

Richee was holding his side at this point, even though he'd heard the story at least a thousand times.

"How did you land?" I asked.

Dick chuckled at that one, too. "Badly," he said. "My first try I kept inching the stick down and the plane didn't want to land. Finally I looked up and saw that I didn't have enough runway, so I pushed the throttle and pulled back on the stick. The second time around I got it down. Boy, that pilot was mad at me. He said, 'I can't keep you from being stupid, but I can give you flying lessons.' And that's how I learned to fly."

Richee continued to laugh at my expression, elbowing Graham in the ribs and covering his mouth as his shoulders bounced up and down. "Tell . . . her . . ." he tried through breaths. "Tell her the one about the barn."

"Oh," Dick said. "A few years later, when I was in the insurance business, I had to fly myself to a meeting, and I was in a hurry, so rather than manually checking the tanks I just checked the logbook to see how much fuel I had." I would later learn that this was a cardinal sin in aviation. You always visually checked your fuel levels before takeoff, because you never knew when a gauge was going to malfunction, or when someone would forget to log their time in a logbook. This was a lesson Dick learned the hard way.

"Anyway," he continued, "someone forgot to log their time in the logbook, and when I was about fifteen minutes from the airport the thing ran out of fuel and the engines sputtered to a stop."

Richee was laughing again, putting his palms up to his aching, flushed cheeks.

"I knew I could coast it in if I could just find a place to land," Dick said. "But ground fog had set in and I couldn't see anything. Finally, I saw what looked like a field, so I took it down. It was a field, and I almost had it on the ground when I looked up and saw a barn right in front of me."

The crew was doubled over now and the breath had left them. Richee's face was crimson and his mouth was open, but nothing would come out.

"At least the doors were open," Dick continued. "I flew the nose of the plane right through the front door. I would have made it, too, if the wings had been a little shorter. They clipped the sides of the barn, and the thing nosed over and flipped. I tore that barn up pretty good and ruined the plane. But I was okay.

"I got out and dusted my suit off, and was looking at the plane when all of a sudden a hand touched my shoulder and somebody said, 'Is he dead?' I nearly jumped out of my skin. It was still pitch black out, so I didn't see the guy coming. It turned out to be the farmer who owned the barn. He'd walked up and assumed, since I was standing there in a suit, I had just wandered into the crash. He figured the pilot had to be dead and I was just there to check things out."

"That's unbelievable," I said.

"Yeah, well, it was pretty believable when I had to pay for that barn. The scariest part of the whole deal was when that guy touched my shoulder. I'd been fine until then. He scared the wits out of me."

On and on it went. More stories, more Tennessee iced tea, and plenty of laughter filled the rest of our day. At that moment I knew I had found a home. I'd been driving for Jack Roush (of Roush Racing) for years and never once had the crew gone out to a meal together. I had learned more about Dick Simon in an hour than I'd ever learned about Jack, and I liked what I saw. This was a family. Dick genuinely cared about everyone who worked with him, and he was one of the most colorful people I'd ever seen. Plus, he owned Indy cars and he wanted to win.

By the time I boarded the plane for the return trip to Ft. Lauderdale my mind was made up. All my efforts would go into Indy car racing. I was hooked. I had no idea how long it would take, but I knew that someday I would race in the Indy 500 for Dick Simon Racing.

PIT STOP

First, be sure to find out what the rules are. Then I believe in playing by the rules and winning by the rules before you consider rewriting the rules. That way you earn respect and credibility and gain supporters. Some situations require you to be forceful, but as long as you don't compromise your principles or your integrity and never lose sight of your goals, you'll achieve them.

End of Chpt. 7

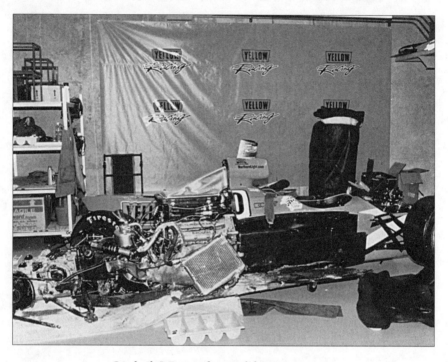

Crashed G Force after qualifying attempt in
Dick Simon Racing garage.
Photo: Courtesy of William J. Ray/Photos by Ray

CHAPTER EIGHT

Chpt. 8 > gres fm pg. 135 to 162 = 28 pgs

IN THE BLINK OF
AN EYE

Indy takes on a new level of excitement on Pole Day, the first day of qualifying, and the 2000 race was no exception. There's electricity in the air as drivers and crews arrive at the track, and the fans are rowdier and more energized than during regular practice sessions. For starters, everybody arrives earlier. The track goes green at 8:00 A.M., and everyone is out early fine-tuning their setups, warming and scrubbing tires, and getting a sense of the track conditions as they prepare for the most important run of the year. This is the start of a two-day make-or-break session where everything has to come together or all the sweat and tears will have been for naught. Nerves are palpable, and conversations are short and clipped. Everybody is on a sharper edge. There are no casual strolls through Gasoline Alley or pit lane. Everything is fast, furious, and frenetic.

Even the Yellow Shirts pick it up a notch for Pole Day, blowing their whistles louder and more often than normal and taking their duties to new extremes. All for good reason: Pole Day is the first true test of May for many of the teams—a day that will determine who stays for the race and who goes home.

The Indy 500 is really two races: the race to qualify and the race itself. Most drivers agree that the first race—the race to get into the race—is the most important of the two. Once you make the field at Indy, you become one of the *chosen,* an Indy 500 Driver. No matter how you finish, the fact that you're in the field puts you in elite company and makes for quite a payday in terms of prize money. In recent history the team finishing last can bring in close to $150,000. Pole Day is the team's first chance to join those ranks.

Unlike other sports where exemptions are given for past champions, and qualification can come in a number of different ways—wins throughout the year, point totals over a certain period, a top finish in the previous year's event—Indy doesn't take past accomplishments into account. Every team qualifies for the Indy 500 in exactly the same way. Beginning on Pole Day, everybody lines up and runs. At the end of two days, the thirty-three fastest cars are in the field. The rest go home. No exceptions. Why thirty-three? The following equation explains where this figure comes from. (Keep in mind that the length of the racetrack is two and a half miles, and that to avoid overcrowding, in 1911 the AAA decided that there should only be one car for every 400 feet of racetrack on the two-and-a-half-mile course.) So, 5,280 feet in a mile times 2.5 miles equals 13,200 feet; divided by 400 feet equals 33.

Roger Penske tucked his tail and went home in 1995 after showing up at Indy with a small army of engineers, technicians, mechanics, cars, and drivers, including the defending champion, Al Unser, Jr., and former 500 winner and world champion Emerson Fittipaldi. I remember watching as the Team Penske trucks and Little Al (as Unser is commonly known) and Emerson emptied their garages and exited the track. That's when it struck me: this place doesn't care who you are or what you've done; if you aren't among the thirty-three fastest, your previous ten victories, including the one you racked up last year, get you nowhere. In 1995 it was "see you next year, Mr. Penske."

In 1997 the Speedway made an exception to their rule, and it turned into such a disaster they quickly abandoned it. With Tony George's newly formed Indy Racing League (IRL) struggling to gain credibility and a national audience, the Speedway, under Tony's leadership, exempted the top-twenty IRL point earners into the field at Indy as long as they qualified. Not only did that decision diminish the impact and importance of Pole Day but it also put Speedway officials in a precarious position. I qualified that year with the sixteenth fastest time, but because of the exemptions, I stood a very good chance of being bumped out of the field.

"What should I do?" I remember asking Ron Hemelgarn, my team owner that year and team owner of the 1996 Indy 500 winner driven by Buddy Lazier.

"Don't worry about it," Ron said. "Just relax, and have a piece of chicken."

That was Ron's answer to everything. He was the most laid-back owner in the garages, a mountain of a man who owned a chain of health clubs and never worried about anything but was as intensely competitive as any team owner I'd ever met.

"Have a piece of chicken?" I said in disbelief. The way I saw it, I stood a better-than-average chance of being the first driver in Indy 500 history to be sent packing after having one of the thirty-three fastest qualifying cars. And Ron wanted me to eat chicken!

"It's really good," Ron said. "Something about the spices they put in the batter really brings out the flavor. You should try some."

"I can't eat chicken right now," I said. "What if I'm bumped?"

Ron shook his head. "You worry too much. That'll give you ulcers." He took another bite from a fried chicken breast. "This sure is good."

Damn the chicken, I thought. I had to know if the Speedway was going to boot the sixteenth fastest car to make room for Tony's IRL point-leaders. I marched out of the garage in a huff and went straight to Leo Mehl's office. Leo was the executive director of the IRL and the former longtime director of worldwide motor sports for Goodyear Tire & Rubber, and a friend. If anybody would have the answers I needed, it would be Leo.

I waited almost half an hour to get into Leo's Gasoline Alley office that afternoon while anxiously convinced I was going to be bumped from the field. When I finally got an audience, the first words out of my mouth were: "Leo, are you taking the fastest thirty-three, or do I need to hustle through the garage and find another car to qualify?"

Leo said, "You know, Lyn, you and I have had a lot of good times together, and it sure is great to have you around during the month of May. I never really wanted you to set that record in Talladega because I thought it would distract you and move your career in another direction. You always belonged in Indy cars. 'Course I guess I was wrong about that. It helped your career, but . . ."

"That's great, Leo," I interrupted. "But I'm running out of time here. The gun goes off in less than two hours, and I've got to know something."

"I know, I know," he said. "It's always this way, isn't it? Remember ninety-two? Now that was a great year."

"Leo . . ."

"Now, now," he said. "You know you've always been one of my favorite people here. I hope you continue to keep an Indianapolis address. Too many of our drivers are moving down South these days, and I'm afraid it's diluting the culture of the city."

It was hopeless. I checked my watch and saw that it was already 4:20, and Leo was prattling on about this and that, bringing up every subject but the one I wanted to discuss. Once it became obvious I was running out of time to get another car, cut a deal, and get fitted safely in the car and get it on the track, I thanked Leo for his time and stormed back to Ron Hemelgarn's garage, where I found Ron with a piece of fried chicken in his hand.

"Would you like a piece of chicken?" Ron asked with a grin. "You might as well wait here because after the six P.M. gun goes off, the IRL is holding a press conference to announce their decision."

We all sat in the garage, clustered around the big-screen TV, waiting for the announcement. Perched on the edge of my chair, I listened as Leo announced that the speedway was expanding the field to thirty-five cars this year so the thirty-three fastest and the IRL qualifiers would all be included.

"Whew," I sighed, bowing my head and letting my shoulders sag.

"I told you not to worry," Ron said. "The Speedway never eats its young. They've always taken the thirty-three fastest cars, and they always will take the thirty-three fastest cars. You could have saved yourself a lot of aggravation if you'd just stayed here and had a piece of this chicken."

I finally ate the chicken, and realized Ron was right on all fronts. The Speedway would always take the thirty-three fastest cars. That was a tradition nobody dared challenge. And he was right about the chicken. The seasoning made it taste great.

Returning to the scene in May 2000, I had a pretty good feeling about our car on Friday. We had gotten enough speed on Tuesday to qualify, but we'd lost it in the subsequent tinkering process, only to get it back late Friday afternoon. You're never completely comfortable leaving the track the night before Pole

Day, but I was as close as you could get. Deb Turner had organized a couple of media events for Friday evening, so I left the garage before knowing our setup for Saturday. I would arrive at sunrise and be ready to qualify the car.

At 6:15 on Friday evening, every entered car sent a representative to the bleachers immediately adjacent to the pagoda (a large center structure along the front straightaway where the media and VIPs watched the race). There, once everyone was seated, officials conducted a blind draw to determine the order of qualifying. If your representative drew the number one, you had the right to be first in line to qualify. If you gave up that right by pulling out of line, you had to wait until everyone else either ran their qualifying laps or passed by pulling out of line. Once every car had been given a chance to qualify in the order of the draw, the track opened up for practice until a car was presented in the qualifying line.

We sent Sara Senske as our draw designee, and Richee Simon drew for Stephan. The whole draw process took no more than half an hour. I wanted Sara to go so she'd learn another tradition at Indy to help her prepare for when she would drive in the race. It worked out for everyone. Sara had a great time chatting with all the team members, and she drew number forty-five for us, which was perfect. There were sixty-five car-and-driver combinations vying for those coveted thirty-three. We didn't have to go out first, but we weren't too far down the list.

Qualifying isn't a race where everybody runs at the same time. Each car attempting to qualify is on the track alone.

After one warm-up lap your next four laps are timed, assuming you take the green flag, and your qualifying speed is the average of those four laps. You can always stop after your warm-up lap if you don't think the car is right, and as long as you don't take the green flag, you won't be charged with an attempt. Assuming you do take the green flag, you can still "wave off" your attempt at any time before the checkered flag falls, but in that case, you are charged with a qualifying attempt. You have only three attempts to qualify. Every time you wave off an attempt, it compounds the pressure to make it on the next run.

Day one of qualifying is called Pole Day because it's the day the pole sitter (the fastest car and the car starting on the inside of row one on race day) is determined. "Pole" is a horse racing term. The "pole position" was always the front, inside position during a horse race, usually marked by a specific pole on the infield fence. Since the first auto races were held on horse tracks, the car with the premium spot on the front inside of the track was said to be in the "pole" position. The name stuck, and soon cars began racing to see who would get to race from the pole position. At Indy, the winner of the pole gets an extra $100,000, so there was more than pride and position at stake on this first qualification day.

I was confident that if the car ran the way it had late Friday and all day on Tuesday we had an excellent chance of making the field and an outside chance of qualifying toward the front. While I'd never been on the front row at Indy, I did qualify in the second row, in sixth place, in 1994, beating out

Mario Andretti and Nigel Mansell, both former world champions. Maybe this was the year? That was a nice thought, but my first priority was qualifying the car. Everything else was secondary.

When I walked outside my apartment on Saturday morning the first words out of my mouth were, "Oh my God it's cold!" A polar blast had moved down from Canada overnight, and at 6:30 A.M. the temperature hadn't hit 45 degrees. I could see my breath, which was something that hadn't happened all month. The Weather Channel confirmed that we had, indeed, had a cold snap overnight, and temperatures were not likely to exceed 60 degrees all day. I needed to get out to the track and get some tires warmed up.

When I got to the track John Martin was already there.

"What will this do to our setup?" I asked. This was the one variable I had feared from the beginning. A car could run great one minute under certain weather conditions, but if the weather changed dramatically, as it had over the previous twelve hours, the car could be an unmanageable piece of junk. John had been saying all week that the soft-spring setup was tough to dial in. Now we had as serious a change in the weather as we'd had all month, and nobody knew what the result was going to be on the car.

"I wish I could tell you," John said. "We're going with the same camber setup as yesterday, but I'm going to start you out with a little less front wing. We need to get the tires warmed up before we put much speed on it, so let's get it out early and see what we've got."

I was with him on that one. We needed to be out on the track as soon as the green flag fell for our group. The first half of the field, those who drew numbers one through twenty-five, had the track to themselves from 8:00 A.M. for thirty minutes of green track time, and the second group, those who drew numbers over twenty-six, which included us, had the track for another thirty minutes. The track then opened for everybody to practice until 10:00 A.M. Then it shut down as the festivities for qualifying got under way. The first car in the order was due on the track at 11:00 A.M., and we had a lot to do between now and then.

We weren't the only team sweating the change in weather conditions. Everybody had the same concerns, and the same ideas. By 7:45 A.M. pit lane looked like a Wal-Mart parking lot. Cars filled every pit box, with golf carts and flatbed buggies scurrying around the pits like bugs on a light. It was going to be a tough morning. The track was likely to be full from the get-go, which meant it would be difficult to get any unencumbered laps in before qualifying began.

We also had a lot of new people in our garage and pit box, but that was always how it worked on Pole Day. This was the weekend the VIPs showed up, and Dick Simon Racing had more than its fair share of those. One was a lanky Texan with thick leathery skin, kinky hair, and a foul mouth. He often annoyed me so I didn't spend a lot of time exchanging pleasantries with him. But he had bought Dick's 18-wheeler at a time when Dick needed all the financial support he could get.

Loyal to a fault, Dick brought him into the fold every year, and every race he waltzed in on race weekend like he owned the place. When I heard him say to Dick, "That soft setup on Lyn's car isn't going to be worth a shit on a morning like this," it was all I could do to bite my tongue. Fortunately I had John around to insulate me from such nonsense.

"What's the plan?" I asked John as we pulled the car onto pit lane.

He shrugged. "Just try to find an opening and let's get some heat in those tires," he said. "I'm putting a quarter-inch wicker on the left front, a one-eighth-inch wicker on the right front, and a one-eighth-inch wicker on the rear wing."

That was a lot of downforce, too much if we expected to dial in the setup in time to qualify on the front row. God had thrown us a real curveball with the weather. Now it was time to see who could scramble and adapt to it best.

Scott Harrington, a thirty-six-year-old from Louisville, Kentucky, was the first out at 8:00, followed by thirty-four-year-old Billy Boat, one of A. J. Foyt's drivers. The third car out belonged to the youngest driver trying to qualify and the driver who had logged more practice laps than anyone: nineteen-year-old Sarah Fisher. Nobody else had put it together yet, but I knew that if Sarah and I both qualified, not only would it be the first time in history two women had ever raced in the Indy 500, but we would also be the youngest and the oldest drivers in the field. "Go get 'em, Sarah," I said to myself.

The yellow flag came out twice during the first thirty minutes, once when Eliseo Salazar's car sprayed liquid all over the track (it turned out to be a water overflow) and a second time when Jimmy Kite pushed his car too quickly and spun out in the grass adjacent to the warm-up lane. Two yellows in half an hour didn't leave much time for the first group to get a lot done, but I had expected as much. This was going to be a rough morning all around.

We went out and back in at 8:35 A.M., taking only one lap and doing nothing more than running a system check. The outside temperature hadn't quite hit 55 degrees yet, and the track was barely 60 degrees and not likely to get much warmer. In addition to cold temperatures, clouds had moved in from the west, which meant there wasn't any radiant sunlight for the asphalt to absorb. Cold tires and a cold track were a bad combination, especially on a day when drivers were anxious to push their cars to the limit. I expected to see a lot of yellows and a few crashes in the morning session. I just hoped nobody got hurt.

The next yellow flag came out at 8:48 A.M. when Eddie Cheever, a former Indy 500 winner and a world-class driver, spun out in the exit of Turn Two. Fortunately, Eddie kept his wits about him, accelerating at precisely the right moment during the spin, and cutting his wheels in just the right way to recover before hitting the wall. A less experienced driver would have locked the car down and slid into the white concrete barricade in front of the Turn Two suites, but Eddie had been around enough years and had experienced enough close calls to know what to do. He brought the car in, and twenty minutes later Eddie ran the fastest lap of the morning, posting a 223.892 on his fourth lap after the near miss.

We were still struggling. I hit the rev limiter in sixth gear along the front straightaway at 212.014 mph, not nearly fast enough to be running those kinds of rpms. I also had a lot of push in the turn entries. I would turn the steering wheel and the car wouldn't respond. The front wheels would turn, but there would be a little skid, a slight hesitation before the tires gripped and the car reacted. It was a minute hesitation, the kind of thing the average person would never notice. But Indy car drivers were trained to believe what their butts told them, and my butt was telling me we had a "pushy" car this morning.

"I'm not comfortable," I told John after a second lap of 219.888. "We're not holding the line, and I'm right up against the rev limiter in the straightaways."

"Yeah, you hit it in the front stretch," John said. "I want you to try the rear sway bar one notch stiffer and let's see if that helps."

"How about a little more front wing?" Dick said over the radio. I didn't see him, but I knew he was behind my car somewhere. Dick was running back and forth between Stephan's pit and mine, monitoring radio transmissions on both cars and keeping his eyes and hands on everything. It amazed me how much energy one man could have. Dick still held the record for having qualified the most cars (seven) in a single race, and he had juggled his duties then just as he was juggling now. I was glad I had John on my crew, but it was also good to know Dick was keeping up with our progress.

"I'll take it up a couple of clicks," John said. "We're still a little colder on the right rear tire than I'd like."

"What are the tire pressures?" Dick asked.

"We've got forty-six on the right front and rear, thirty-seven on the left front, and thirty-eight on the left rear."

I could see Dick now. He had walked around the back of the car and was eyeballing my front wing. "That's okay," he said. "A couple of clicks and a little stiffer rear sway bar should do it."

Unlike your street car where the suspension sway bar is usually pretty small, thus giving you that smooth, boatlike feeling as you drive, Indy cars are stiff while maintaining as much mechanical grip as possible. To get that balance, we have two knobs that adjust the stiffness of the front and rear sway bars. The stiffer the bar, which was what we were going with, the less the car is able to roll in the turns.

We went back out at 9:22 A.M. and I ran a couple of laps in the 219 range, but the changes weren't working. I couldn't hold the throttle flat through the apex, and my lines were too shallow through the turns. If there is any track where you simply cannot overdrive the car, it's the Indianapolis Motor Speedway. The turns have to be long and fluid, and you have to be patient. Your mind tricks you, telling you you're in the apex of the turn when you still have several feet to go. You have to wait patiently through the apex so you can gain momentum coming off the turn. I wasn't able to do that with the setup we had. We needed to get some of the downforce off the rear of the car.

"Come on, guys," I said after pitting at 9:45 A.M. "We're running out of time here."

"Still got fifteen minutes," I heard Sara say over the radio. She was working as a spotter in Turn Three, and I couldn't have asked for a better person for that job. Not only could Sara Senske keep me updated on traffic through Turns Two, Three, and Four and the back straightaway, she was a driver, so she could spot subtleties in the car that others might miss. She noticed the downforce problem in the apex of Turn Three the same time I was feeling it in my butt. "You're looking a little pushy," she had said. "I think you've got too much downforce." Now she was providing a calming voice, telling me we still had fifteen minutes of practice time, plenty of time to dial in the setup before the checkered flag fell and qualifying began.

"Let's back off that sway bar about fifty percent," Dick said after I stopped.

John nodded his agreement. "Yeah, and I'm going to replace this eighth with a one-sixteenth wicker on the rear, and add five clicks to the front wing."

That should take care of the downforce. We'd run enough laps now that I wasn't as concerned about the cold tires as I was about the push we were getting. If we could get the setup a little more neutral, we might have it. But whatever we did, we needed to hurry.

"Ten minutes," Steve Melson said over the radio. We needed to get out of the pits.

"How much fuel?" Dick asked.

There was a long pause as our telemetry technician, the guy John described as "needing a lot of curing before going to the barrel," fumbled through the data for our current fuel level.

"It should be . . . Here it is," he said. "We've got seven and a half gallons."

"Okay," Dick said, although I could tell from the slightly higher pitch in his voice that he was getting anxious. "Let's get a couple of good laps in before ten."

Nobody had to answer. John made one final visual check of the wing angles, and Steve gave me the thumbs-up. Gary Green, Steve, and John pushed the car out of the pit box and I sped down the warm-up lane.

"You've got one flier on the outside," the Turn-One spotter said as I ran through the gears. "Looking good after that."

"Looks good," Sara said as I came onto the track at the exit of Turn Two. I wasn't sure if she meant the track or the car or both, but I knew if I had some traffic problems she would let me know.

My first lap was only 210.625, but I could tell the car was better. As I passed the start-finish line I had a good feeling about the lap I was about to run. The car held perfectly through Turn One, and I could tell it was quicker. The short chute was on me before I knew it, and I was already setting up for Turn Two. The changes had been just right, and this lap was going to be a good one.

"Looks great," Sara said. That was all I needed to hear.

When I entered the front straightaway from Turn Four I knew this would be my last lap. Once we had the car we wanted, there was no reason to risk another run. I blew past the start-finish line and pressed the button for the radio as I headed back into Turn One. "Coming in," I said.

"Roger that, Lyn," Steve said. "Coming in."

I'd run 222.113, a speed I thought might be good enough to qualify in the front row. That was it. The car was right. Now all we had to do was put four of those laps together during qualifying.

For more than fifty years, the public address announcer for the Indianapolis Motor Speedway has been a fellow named Tom Carnegie, who, even though he was well into his eighties, had a rumbling baritone voice that reminded me of what Moses must have sounded like when addressing the seven tribes. At 10:45 A.M. I heard that voice over the speakers saying: "Aaaaaand, they're coming down the front stretch. It's . . . three-time Indianapolis 500 winner Johnny Rutherford!"

Johnny was turning the ceremonial first laps in the Chaparral he drove to victory in 1980, and Carnegie, in his way, made it sound like the most exciting moment in sports. Right behind Johnny was 1963 Indy 500 winner Parnelli Jones, one of the last true mavericks of the sport and a man whose name had been used by more state troopers than any other driver in America—"Goin' a little fast there, son. Who do you think you are, Parnelli Jones?" Well, the real Parnelli Jones was going slowly around the track today as he waved to fans at every turn. It was an Indy tradition, and one I enjoyed watching, no matter how much pressure we were under.

After hauling the car back to the garage to check the cross-weights and add fuel since no fuel was allowed in the pits during qualifying, we got in line according to the draw for the final tech inspection before qualifying.

It was still colder than an Irish midnight, and I wondered what sorts of early lap times we might get out of this weather. At 11:00 A.M. when Buzz Calkins took the track, the air temperature was 51, and the track temp was 69 degrees. Not surprisingly, Buzz waved off after turning two laps at a 217.292 average. Little Al Unser was next out. His four laps were 218.187; 220.248; 221.326; and 221.440, for an average of 220.293. Any average over 220 stood a reasonable chance of remaining in the field, and Al had to feel pretty good about his run. Each lap was better than the previous one, and he had run all four laps in two minutes, forty-three seconds, a solid start and a good number to post early.

Little Al's cousin Robby Unser waved off after failing to get above 218 in his first two laps. Then Eddie Cheever qualified his backup car with a time of 221.270. Robbie Buhl took the early lead five minutes later with a four-lap average of 221.357.

Three cars had gone all four laps and each car had run faster than the one before it. It looked like teams had adjusted well to the changing weather. The day was young, but it looked like it might take a speed of 224 to win the pole.

The first crash of qualifying came at 11:27 A.M. when Jimmy Kite hit the outside wall of Turn One during his warm-up lap. The car spun backward in the apex and Jimmy had no chance to recover. The left rear wheel hit the wall first, sending suspension pieces flying. Then the left front wheel hit, sending more debris in the air, and the tub skidded along the edge of the wall until it came to a stop. Jimmy climbed from the car before the track ambulance and emergency team arrived, and doctors at the track medical center released him and cleared him to drive within the hour. It wasn't a bad accident, just the first of the day. It reminded everybody that this was not a time to lose focus, even for a second. The slightest hiccup, even on a warm-up lap, could lead to disaster.

Debris was cleared off the track, oil dry was sprinkled in strategic spots, and the track reopened in less than ten minutes. At 11:42 A.M. Jason Leffler qualified with a 220.417 average, and ten minutes later, Jeff Ward put together the four most consistent laps of the day, averaging 222.636 with only one-twentieth of a second separating his fastest and slowest laps.

But there was no time for anyone else to ponder Ward's consistency. The second he came off the track, Sarah Fisher took her first warm-up lap in Indy qualifying. She had received a lot of press because of her age and the fact that she was attempting to become only the third woman to qualify for the Indy 500. Two minutes and forty-three seconds later, Ms. Fisher took the checkered flag, having qualified her car with a four-lap average speed of 220.237 mph.

Although we were busy, I took a little time to watch Sarah's run, and I caught myself smiling as she took the checkered flag. The girl had talent and confidence to burn. In a few minutes I would be her competitor again, but for a second or two, I wanted to enjoy the moment and relish what Sarah had done. I felt like a proud aunt.

Tom Carnegie called Sarah over for a chat on the track PA system, and she was as effervescent as I would have expected her to be. Moses put his big octogenarian arm around her and said, "SSSSarah Fisher, ladies and gentlemen, only nine . . . teen . . . years . . . old, and in her first Indianapolis 500 she has qualified the number fifteen Walker Racing Cummins Special with an average qualifying speed of two . . . hundred . . . twenty . . . point . . . two . . . three . . . seven miles per hour. Sarah, how does it feel?"

"Well, I was a little anxious before I got in," Sarah said with a slight giggle. "But once you get on the track, your focus comes in. I was wide open on the straightaways, so that was all she had. The worst seems to be over now. We just need to work now on our hot-condition setup because we're lacking a little in that. Our cold-condition setup is actually much better."

"So, how was the car during that spec . . . tacular run?" Tom asked, seemingly oblivious to the setup analysis Sarah had just given.

"Oh, the car was as good as it was going to get without a little more scrub," she said, falling right into Tom's cadence. "It was a little better this morning, but for the time of day and conditions we ran, it was great."

No, she was great. Sarah had come a long way since her days as a precocious fifteen-year-old in my driver development program. Now she had qualified for the Indy 500 as the youngest rookie in the field. I felt a warm glow of pride inside, but I had to shake my head to clear the emotion and get ready to go to work.

The next seven cars out waved off, and nobody cracked the 220 mark on a single lap. I was the eighth car in line after the track reopened. Sara Senske had come down from Turn Three to watch my qualifying run. Since you qualify alone on the track, there was no reason to have a spotter in Turn Three, and Sara wanted to be close to the action. Dick invited her to follow him down to the flag station, an area in the small alley between the inside wall of the track and the outside wall of pit lane, where crew members either waved the driver off or gave the go-ahead to take the checkered flag. The alley was also known as the "trough," an affectionate nickname that accurately described the area. At any point during the run, a team representative in the trough could throw the yellow flag to signal a wave-off. Dick was always in the trough when one of his cars was running. It was just another gesture of kindness when he invited Sara to join him.

My husband, Roger, was also in the trough. Sara, Dick, and the Speedway official filled out the crowd at the flag station as I exited the pits. If nothing else, it would be an interesting run.

From the moment I hit the back straightaway, I knew the car wasn't ready. It felt sluggish, almost as though the fuel mixture was too lean. We had taken most of the downforce out a little earlier, so I didn't expect it to feel like I was pulling a trailer, but that's exactly how it felt. I might just as well have had a parachute behind the car. Maybe it would get better during the warm-up lap, but I doubted it.

My first lap was 217.649, which was nowhere close to being fast enough. Unless I got substantially faster my second time around, we would have to wave off. Dick held up the yellow flag and waved me back into the pits.

"Aaaaaannnd, there's the yellow flag," Carnegie said over the speakers. "The number ninety Dick Simon Racing–Yellow Freight System car driven by Lyn St. James has waved off. That's the first attempt for the number ninety car."

The track opened for practice between 2:00 and 3:30. Nobody presented a car during that time, but we weren't ready to take advantage of the practice. The car was in the garage, and John and Steve were going over the telemetry readings and set up sheets, searching for the magic formula that would squeeze us above the 220 mph mark.

Five more cars qualified between 3:30 and 3:55, with Greg Ray, a slick boy from Plano, Texas, setting the mark with a four-lap average of 223.471. After Greg took the checkered flag, Jeret Schroeder waved off after two laps that barely topped 219. It was Schroeder's second unsuccessful attempt. He had only one more try to get in.

The track opened up again for practice at 4:03 when no cars were presented. This time we were ready. I sped out of the pits the moment the track went green, and knew we had done the right thing. The first lap was only 208.478, but a lap later I got up to 216.711 in traffic. The car was much smoother. We had taken most of the downforce out and were running a negative wing angle and no wicker. This was it. I could qualify this car. We hustled back to the garage, put in 10 gallons of fuel, and took one more peek at the cross-weights before putting the car in line for tech inspection. Meanwhile Stephan was having problems of his own. At 4:40, only twenty minutes before Happy Hour and eighty minutes before the gun went off closing the first day of qualifying, Stephan ran two laps that didn't sniff 220. His best was 219.394, not enough to ensure a spot in the field. After the second lap, Dick, still standing in the trough with his radar gun and flags, threw the yellow and waved off another attempt. That was two attempts for Stephan. The next time he took the green he would either qualify the car or go home.

As Happy Hour began, the already frenetic pace picked up even more. Clouds still blanketed the sky, but the track had warmed a little. We'd had all day to dial in the setup and get accustomed to the conditions. Now it was time to show everybody what we had.

Stephan went back out at 5:21, two cars ahead of me, but he never finished his warm-up lap. Dick threw the yellow when it became apparent that the car wasn't up to speed. It was a close call. If Stephan had taken the green flag and tried to stretch out a speed that wasn't there, he could have failed to qualify. As it was, the wave-off before the green did not count as an attempt. Stephan still had one try left, but only forty minutes to get it done.

"Okay, Lyn," John said. "I've got zero wicker and negative one degree on the rear wing."

I gave him the thumbs-up. We'd been through tech, so no more changes were allowed. It was qualify this setup or give up our chance at the pole and wait until tomorrow to try to bump our way into the field, a prospect I didn't even want to consider.

Roberto Guerrero, a great guy who lived near Dick in San Juan Capistrano, California, went out at 5:24 but waved off after three progressively slower laps. The moment Roberto pulled into the pits, we fired the starter.

"Let's go! Let's go!" Steve shouted.

I screeched out of the pits and ran through the gears as quickly and efficiently as I could, checking the gauges and temperatures as I entered the back straightaway and feeling the car as I entered Turn Three. This was better than a good one; we had finally hit it just right.

"Go get 'em, kiddo," Dick said as I passed the start-finish line and began my warm-up lap. He and Sara were back at the flag station with Roger, and John had made it down this time. It wouldn't have mattered who was there. I was focused on the run; and the run was one flat-out solid piece of work. This could be my best Indy qualifying run yet.

"Oh, shit," Dick said as I exited Turn Four on my warm-up lap. "We're going for the pole!"

My warm-up was 221, and I was getting faster by the second. I was flat-footed all the way and the car handled beautifully. We had a chance! If I held it together, we could be on the pole!

Turn One was on me, and I set it up just the way I wanted,

picking my markers and initiating the turn at exactly the right spot. The line was right there in front of me, a nice, long sweeping arc, just like Dick had shown me years before, and just as I had done a thousand times in the previous nine years. The apex came right where it should, and the car felt wonderful as it held the loads. I was almost through the turn, and then it would be into the short chute and a quick setup for Turn Two.

Then in an instant, a nanosecond, not even enough time for the brain to process what was happening, the rear wheels spun around. It wasn't a gradual spin or a loose feeling that I had time to react to; it was a whip; an instant malfunction that sent the car into a complete spin toward the inside of the track. It had come late, too late, really. I was already past the apex. The loads should have been diminishing. The car should have held easily. But I didn't have time to think about those things. All I could do at that point was hang on.

The first impact with the inside wall demolished the right side of the car and sent both right-side wheels flying through the air. I would later learn from track officials that the black box, the computer monitor all cars kept on board to measure the effects of crashes, showed an impact of 60 g's. One "g" is the equivalent force of your body weight pressing against you as momentum or gravity takes hold. If you go around a curve on the highway a little too fast in your street car, or if you take a circular exit ramp off the interstate at a slightly less-than-comfortable speed, you'll probably pull about a half of a "g," or half the gravity load of your body weight. F-18 fighter pilots pull as many as 9 g's during maneuvers, but anything above that requires them to wear g-suits, special pressurized flight suits that control the loads applied to the body. There were no tests or comparisons for a 60 g impact. What I was experiencing was unique to racing. But I wasn't through yet.

The first conscious thought I remember having was, "Oh my God, I'm in the air. I'm going over." The car was airborne and listing hard to the right. I was sure it was about to tip over, and I was going to land on my head with a force I didn't want to imagine. I couldn't move in the cockpit, but in my mind, at least, I was leaning with all I had, trying to will that car back over to an upright position. Somehow—I still don't know how—the car came back from a 50-degree angle to land on the track upright.

The slap from that impact measured 40 g's, enough force to jar everything loose that hadn't already come off. But I was still spinning. The car then slid across the track and spun another half turn until I hit the outside wall with a force that measured 50 g's. Finally the car ground to a stop at an angle in the middle of the track. I was stunned and winded, but I was conscious. I was alive! Adrenaline was pumping at full force, so I wasn't sure what sort of injuries I might have sustained. I felt fine, but you never know.

I took off the steering wheel and laid it on top of the tub, a sign to emergency crews that I was conscious and coherent enough to follow procedure. They would be there with the ambulance in a matter of seconds, I knew. Indy emergency personnel were the best in the business. They would have me checked out and on my way to the trackside medical center in under two minutes.

"Lyn, can you hear me?" I heard one of the medical technicians say.

I nodded as I unbuckled my seat belts and helmet snaps and the emergency crew unhooked the headrest. Medical workers were on both sides of me now, helping me get out of the car. Nothing was broken, or so I thought. I'd broken my wrist once in a crash, and I'd been in racing long enough to identify different types of injuries by feel. I hurt in several places, and I was dizzy from the jarring impacts, but other than that I appeared to be fine.

Then it hit me.

I was done. In the blink of an eye, I'd gone from contending for the pole to being carted off to the trackside medical center. All the work, all the time, all the sponsor calls, the tears, the sweat, the deal making, the focus, the intensity, the preparation, and the man-hours on the track and in the garage had just blown up in my face in less than a second.

This was it. I was through. As I sat in the ambulance, my helmet in hand, my heart and my head both sank. At that moment I was sure that my 2000 Indy racing experience was over. And my career as an Indy car driver lay strewn in a thousand pieces between the inside and outside walls at the exit off Turn One.

End of chpt 8

chpt 8

Crash with Buddy Lazier during practice at the 1996 Indy Race
at Phoenix International Raceway.
Photo: Courtesy of Bruce Miller

CHAPTER NINE

Chpt. 9 → gres frm pg. 163 to 182 = (30 pgs)

PRESSING AHEAD

Race car drivers don't talk about crashes. It's taboo, a forbidden subject that isn't even discussed privately among ourselves in the secure confines of drivers' meetings. Any conversations about the wrecks we've personally experienced or the feelings we have gone through when friends have crashed are kept inside, not to be shared with anyone. Family, friends, and fellow drivers know better than to broach the subject. It's like the crazy aunt who lives in the attic; race car drivers go through their careers with the knowledge that they could be seriously injured or killed doing what they do, but it's a subject they rarely openly discuss. No one is immune. The world's best drivers can do everything exactly as they should and still end up in a crash. None of us believe we are going to crash, and nobody in the sport views crashing as inevitable, but we also know that if you put your butt in a race car you have to accept that you might crash. We all know it. We just don't talk about it.

To those of us who have analyzed our own reluctance—and I'm afraid that's a small number in the driving community— the reasons for our reticence are simple and straightforward. Our job requires us to push a car to its limits, to run our bodies and the machine we are driving on a finely sharpened edge. Any negative thoughts, any hesitations, any fears that inhibit us from peak performance have to be stuffed away in the recesses of our minds, otherwise we might as well hang up our helmets and take up golf.

We don't talk about crashes because to do so would require us to think about them, and to think about them means conjuring negative images in our minds. Those memories and the emotions that go with crashes must be locked away in an area of the brain we don't readily access. If they aren't, if we let ourselves dwell on the emotional and physical toll a crash takes, then we can't be at our best when we climb into that race car.

Everybody has negative thoughts in their lives. When you have to deal with stress, you try to leave it behind you and not carry it around with you.

Stopping negative thoughts is a skill every athlete, particularly race car drivers, must master in order to reach the top. You've seen it in other sports. In a close game, Michael Jordan never thought back on the hundreds of shots he'd missed in his life. In the heat of the moment Jordan probably couldn't tell you when he'd ever missed a game-winner at the buzzer. The only memories in his mind were the game-winners he'd made, the shots he'd thrown down at the buzzer, the thousands of times he had come through in the clutch. By the time the actual shot came around, Jordan was convinced he couldn't miss.

Other athletes are the same. Tiger Woods's greatest asset over the rest of the golfers in the world is his belief that he can do the things he does. When other golfers look at 220-yard shots over water to pins cut right on the edges of the greens, they think about how hard the shot is. Woods thinks about holing it from the fairway. That's his gift, and it's what separates him from his competitors.

Champion race car drivers think only in positive terms. It's not, "I don't want to hit the wall"; it's, "I'm going to drive a perfect lap, get the most out of the car, and use all the track."

Each individual has his or her own way of erasing negative thoughts and focusing on positive outcomes. I use what I call the Five Rs of negative thought stopping. These five cues give me the power to control my thinking and frame every experience in its most positive light.

1. RECOGNIZE. Before you can change a negative thought, you have to recognize the fact that you are having it. By increasing your awareness you are better able to control your own thoughts.

2. REFUSE. Don't let the negative thought win. You have to diligently insist that you aren't going to con-

166 written as handwritten note top left.

tinue your negative thinking and stop it in its tracks. This can be done through mental exercises or even defined actions like snapping a rubber band on your wrist every time you have a negative thought to remind yourself to stop it.

3. RELAX. Negative thinking creates anxiety, which leads to tension. The best way to combat that tension is to consciously work on relaxing. There's a reason you see star athletes closing their eyes and taking deep breaths before a crucial point or play or series. They're using this technique to relax.

4. REFRAME. It's virtually impossible to be thought-free. Your mind will fill any void with thoughts. It's up to you to make those thoughts positive. You do this by telling yourself things like, "I've been here before. I've done this before, and I know I can do it again. This is the journey I have chosen, and I am in control."

5. RESUME. With your new, positive frame of reference you should press ahead with a sense of confidence and control.

The craft of putting negatives behind me and pressing ahead was something I had to learn early in my career. It is a learned craft, by the way, not a natural skill. But it is a craft I didn't completely understand or fully appreciate until much later in life.

The first incident in my racing career that forced me to learn to remove negative thoughts came in 1976 at the

Palm Beach International Raceway. It was a Saturday, and I had brought my Irish setter, Max, who was like a member of my family, to the track for the weekend. Max hated being on a leash, so after the track shut down I would take him on a run around the track where he could have plenty of room but also be safe from pedestrian traffic. I think I enjoyed his little romps as much as he did. The hair of his coat looked like feathers as he galloped in the breeze, and it always warmed my heart to see him prancing around the track. That Saturday was no different. He looked beautiful out there.

Then I saw the car. A group of kids had gotten out on the track and were where they were not allowed. I waved and yelled, trying to signal to the driver that a dog was on the track, but it was no use. I closed my eyes just before it happened, but that didn't muffle the thud or the yelp as the car clipped Max in the hindquarters, spinning him off the track and leaving him in a helpless heap. I yelled for them to go back to the paddock and get help. We took Max to a veterinary emergency center, but it was too late. Despite some Herculean efforts by the staff of veterinarians, Max died early the next morning.

I had never wept so hard in my life. I just wanted to go home, lock myself in my bedroom, and stay under the covers forever.

The decision to race that Sunday was one of the hardest I had ever made. The last place I wanted to be was on the racetrack where Max had been killed, but I knew that if I was going to be a race car driver I had to park my emotions and get on with the business at hand. During my warm-up lap, I felt a lump in my throat when I passed the spot on the track where Max had been killed, and for one fleeting moment I thought about packing it in. Then my competitive instincts took over. I locked my emotions and my thoughts about Max in a safe place in the back of my mind, and I focused on the race in front of me. I would remove my feelings because that's what I had to do in order to get behind the wheel on Sunday. It was a hard lesson, but one that would carry me through grave tragedies during the rest of my career.

Crashes are a little different, but the same principles of removing negative memories apply. One of the questions I'm frequently asked at seminars is: "What does it feel like to crash a race car?" The obvious, glib answer to that is, "It hurts." But I know that's not what is really being asked. Most people who have never been inside a race car want to know about the emotions of a crash. They want to know what you feel, how you react, and what goes through your mind as you're hurtling toward a wall at 200 mph. There are no simple answers to those questions.

Crashes are, for the most part, unemotional experiences. You park your emotions when you're driving a race car. That's difficult for those outside of racing to understand, but it's true. For one thing, crashes happen too fast, and you aren't in control, so there is no time for emotion. You simply hang on and prepare yourself for what's coming. Once you've been through a few crashes you learn to let it happen. That sounds silly, but it's vital. You increase your chance of injury when you tense during a crash, locking your arms on the steering wheel or bracing yourself by tightening various muscles. If you remain as loose as possible and stay erect, you have a better chance of walking away with less critical injuries.

After the crash is when the first emotional responses set in. The first feeling is helplessness. I've always said, in answer to those seminar questions, that it feels like someone has just cut off your arms and legs. You want to continue to run, to go, to do what you were just doing, but you can't. Adrenaline is still surging through your system and your mind is still racing. Every sense is on heightened alert and your competitive juices are still flowing when suddenly . . . *Whap!* . . . you're done, you're through, you aren't going anywhere. You feel eviscerated. You've just gone from having nerves explode at every turn to being stopped, helpless, stagnant, quiet, still.

The first big crash I had was in the 1978 Paul Revere 250 at the Daytona International Speedway. The race started at midnight, under the lights, the night before the NASCAR Firecracker 400, and it was, by far, the biggest race I had entered to date. I couldn't wait to jump into John Carusso's Corvette and make a name for myself at Daytona, the king of racetracks in America. Since it was a 250-mile race, it required two drivers, and I was driving with John, my husband at the time. During my stint we had a long yellow and you could tell everyone was getting antsy. The track went green and all hell broke loose. Cars spun everywhere and the infield was soon littered with them. One car spun in front of me and came to a stop in the kink, leaving me nowhere to go. I t-boned the car, centering the nose of the Corvette on its right-side door. All four wheels of my car left the ground and, for a moment, I thought I might flip over onto the hood of the other car. Then I landed with a thud; the entire front half of the Corvette smashed like an accordion.

The first thing I tried to do was restart the car, even though there was steam spewing from what was left of the hood. When the emergency team arrived with the tow truck, I remember being overwhelmed with emotion, shouting to them, "Come on, let's get this thing back to the pit. I know the crew can fix it and we can get it back on the track."

They looked at me as if I were delirious. "Lady," one of them finally said, "this car is never going to turn another wheel."

That's when I first experienced the sensation of total help-lessness. I felt crippled, like I'd been tackled, bound, and gagged while running a marathon. It was a feeling I would never forget, and one I would never grow accustomed to, even though I would experience it several more times in my career.

Certainly the most spectacular crash, if not the worst, I've ever experienced came in 1986 in the IMSA Camel GT Series race at Riverside International Raceway in California. Coming through Turn One at over 180 mph, I was hit from behind by a driver named Doc Bundy. The contact wasn't intentional, it was just aggressive racing, but the results were catastrophic. My car hit a third car, and all three cars became missiles. I hit the pit wall, flipped, spun, and slid upside down on the edge of the track. I remember seeing dirt, gravel, and oil spray over the windshield, and for a split second I thought I was plowing a ditch in the earth. I'd never seen so much debris on a windshield. That was before I saw and felt the fire.

The car ignited, bursting into flames as it continued to skid along the perimeter of the track. When it finally stopped, the entire car was engulfed in fire, with flames leaping from all directions. Still, I was eerily calm throughout the whole ordeal. I hit the fire extinguisher, released my seat belts, unlatched the door, and crawled out through the fire, saying over and over again "don't breathe" so I wouldn't inhale the flames, smoke, or chemicals. I then walked as quickly as possible away from the burning vehicle.

Emergency crews were already on the scene, and they were stunned to see me emerge from the flame ball that was once my car. I was moving as fast as I could, given the two herniated disks I had in my neck, but on tape it looked like I was casually strolling out of the inferno. I could hear the crowd cheering as I emerged, but my main thought was smashing Doc in the face. After being checked out at the infield medical center I drove myself to the local hospital for further X rays. The race was televised, and I was sure my mother had seen the crash. It's odd how the mind works. My only emotion at that moment was worry because I didn't want Mom thinking I was more seriously injured than I was.

After the Riverside crash, I learned another lesson about stopping negative thoughts. The next weekend we were scheduled to race at Laguna Seca, and while I was in no shape to race, the team asked me if I wanted to be there to take a couple of laps in the sister car. I said, "Yes."

After getting strapped into the cockpit I was heading down pit lane to merge onto the track when I had a flashback. Just before I entered the track I saw all the dirt and debris from the Riverside crash rushing across my windshield again. "No!" I said. "Stop that!" I shook my head and moved my hand in a wiping motion in front of my face. It was as if I were cleaning the windshield, erasing the memories of the Riverside crash that were now so vividly in front of me.

It worked. I literally wiped the slate clean, and went on to drive a few laps. From then on I used that technique to control my thoughts. When I had a negative memory—a crash or a bad run—I simply erased it and replaced it with the positive images.

When I realized what a great tool my eraser was for keeping my mind uncluttered and focused on the moment, I developed other, similar techniques for negative thought stopping. Because I was a former secretary, I created an imaginary file cabinet in my head, and whenever an event occurred that needed to be stored out of sight, I would put the thoughts in an imaginary file folder, open the proper drawer, and file the folder away for safekeeping. When I needed to recall the details of the incident, I simply went to my mental filing cabinet, found the correct file, and recalled the memories. Any other time, the bad thoughts were filed in the file cabinet.

Later in my career, when I started working with HPI, I realized that my homegrown filing system had a firm base in sports psychology, and they taught me the Five Rs. All high achievers, no matter what their discipline, have some mental system for focusing on the positive side of their thoughts and not the negative.

I also learned that dealing with the emotional residue from your own crashes is much easier than dealing with tragedies that befall others. From my earliest days in racing I had seen serious injury and death. In one of my early amateur races a driver was killed when his car flipped and landed in a canal. The driver drowned before divers could save him. I remember feeling terrible for this person's family, even though I didn't know them, and I had never met the driver. In an attempt to show support to the family, I walked up to his wife after the race and said, "I don't know you, and I didn't know your husband, but I'm a race car driver. And I can tell you without a doubt that your husband died doing what he loved." I'm sure it was small consolation for the loss of a loved one, but the woman thanked me, and we briefly embraced. If my words helped a little, even if she didn't recall them until much later in the grieving process, it was worth it. But I still didn't understand the toll a tragedy like that takes on your emotions. It took the loss of someone I knew to bring that message home.

By 1996 I considered myself an established Indy 500 driver, not quite as senior a veteran as some, but more established than others. I'd been in crashes and I'd seen plenty of other drivers crash. But nothing could have prepared me for the news I got after leaving the track during the second week of practice, just three days after Pole Day.

I usually never left the track, even when we weren't running. If my car was in the garage, I stayed nearby. It was my rule to be at the track by 9:00 A.M. and stay until 6:00 P.M. You never knew when your team might need you, and I didn't want to become known as a prima donna who showed up only when it was time to drive the car. So it was odd that I left that day. I should have been there—I normally would have been there—but I had a request to speak at a function that benefited the Arthritis Foundation. I figured it wouldn't hurt to leave for an hour or two. While I was gone, Scott Brayton, the pole sitter for that year's Indy 500, was killed in a crash while practicing.

I was devastated. Scott and I had been friends and fellow competitors since before I had raced at Indy, and he was someone I respected and genuinely liked. A funny guy with a wonderful wife, Becky, and a beautiful little daughter, Scott held the world by the tail when he was driving an Indy car. Suddenly, he was gone. And the rest of us, his friends, were left to deal with the anguish of the loss while getting ready to race in the upcoming Indy 500.

We were scheduled to scrub in some tires for the race, but I hadn't reconciled my emotions from Scott's death. I wasn't ready to get in the car. Should I tell the team I needed some time? Or should I go ahead and gut it out? If I did say I wasn't ready to drive, what would my team think? Would I be seen as a wimp, or worse yet, an emotional female? It was one of my more anguished moments at the Speedway, so I needed some advice. I headed to the Goodyear garage to find Leo Mehl. At the time Leo was Goodyear's head of motor sports operations. He would later become the executive director of the IRL, but he would always remain a dear friend of mine.

I confided my feelings to Leo, and I explained my dilemma. "Leo, I know I should drive the car today, but I don't feel comfortable. I haven't come to terms with Scott's death yet, and . . ."

"Then don't do it," Leo said.

"But . . ."

"No buts," he said. "If you go out in that car when you're not ready you're not doing yourself or your team any good. In fact you're taking an unnecessary risk. If you don't feel like driving, say so, and don't. Do it tomorrow and you'll be fine."

I followed Leo's advice, telling the team I wasn't ready to drive the car that day. To a man they all understood. The following day, after I had gone through all my feelings for Scott Brayton and neatly filed them into one of the drawers in my mental cabinet, I drove the car without a moment's hesitation. No one ever said a critical word about my decision not to drive that first day. If anything, I think I gained a measure of respect from some of my teammates because of my discipline and honesty.

Crashes often leave marks that extend far beyond the racetrack. You need only look at the huge national grief and emotional outpouring that occurred after the death of Dale Earnhardt during the 2001 Daytona 500 to see the impact a crash can have on people outside the small enclave of racing.

The most profound example of that in my career came in 1995 when at Turn One of lap one of the Indy 500 I was one of eight drivers embroiled in a horrific crash. We weren't going that fast. In fact, having just taken the green flag, our speed was around 150 mph, but because all thirty-three drivers had just come off the pace laps, we were bunched together. I was on the inside near the back of the pack and couldn't see what had happened ahead of me, but I wasn't alone. Years later, after thousands of analysts examined tapes of the crash, nobody is really sure what happened. All we know is Eddie Cheever and Stan Fox somehow came together, setting off a chain reaction of hitting, sliding, and spinning in all directions.

Most of the action was ahead of me, so I had time to react. I thought I'd found a hole to weave my way through the carnage, but my left front tire clipped the right rear tire of my teammate Carlos Guerrero. In an instant I was in the wall, tangled with a half dozen other drivers in a mass of flying debris. I was fine. In fact, it was one of the least spectacular crashes I'd had as an Indy car driver. What I didn't know at the time was how bad things were for Stan Fox.

Stan's car had been hit at an odd angle. The car had ridden up on another car before climbing the wall and breaking in half. When it hit the track again, Stan's legs were dangling outside of what was left of the tub, and the remainder of his car was trailing at some distance. I didn't see much of the crash firsthand, but I watched the replay enough times to know that it didn't look good.

My suspicions were confirmed by the grim looks at the trackside medical center. Finally I questioned several nurses and Dr. Henry Bock, the track's medical director and chief physician.

"How's Stan?" I asked.

No one would answer.

"Is he alive?"

Dr. Bock finally said, "They've airlifted him to Methodist"—Indianapolis Methodist Hospital, where all track patients were taken for extensive injuries or for observation—"it's pretty grave."

The Speedway doesn't announce deaths during the race, but most of those in attendance assumed Stan hadn't made it. He underwent extensive surgery, including several procedures to drain fluid and relieve swelling from his brain. As the race progressed and I was released from the trackside facility, nobody knew Stan's status.

That included my daughter, who had watched the crash from one of Dick's infield hospitality tents. Lindsay had been sitting with Michelle Marquis, another graduate from my driver development program and the person most instrumental in the creation of the Lyn St. James Driver Development Program. Michelle was a talented driver who had gone to work as an engineer at Chrysler after graduating from Kettering University. That year at Indy she was running errands, keeping track of my schedule, and sitting with Lindsay during the race. The two of them were devastated by the crash. They rushed to the medical center and waited for me to be released after I was fully checked out and cleared. In the meantime, an erroneous rumor filtered to them that Stan had died. When I finally walked out the exit door of the medical facility, Lindsay was standing outside in tears.

"Honey, it's all right," I said. "I'm okay."

"But Mom," she said through sobs, "what about Stan? I heard he died."

My heart sank. This poor young girl had just seen her mother in a terrible crash, one in which more than one driver could have easily been killed, and now she was having to deal with an unsubstantiated rumor that a man she knew had died as a result of his injuries.

All I could do was be honest with her. "It doesn't look good, sweetheart," I said. "But he was alive when they airlifted him to Methodist, and until we hear differently, we have to go on the assumption that he is still alive. All we can do is pray for him and know that he's getting all the help he needs."

We had a good, long hug. At that moment I wanted to hold her forever. Lindsay had lost one mother. The thought of losing another may have been too much for her to bear.

We became much more open in our conversations after that, speaking at length about the perils of what I did for a living and her feelings about life and loss. It was a life-changing moment for the two of us, and one I will never forget.

Lindsay and I visited Stan's family in the hospital, and when Lindsay realized that Stan's daughter, Marie, was her age, I suggested that Lindsay write Marie a letter. All the focus was on Stan and the adults, so I thought it was a good idea for the kids to share their perspectives. Lindsay and Marie shared letters for some time afterward.

Stan never fully recovered. He regained his motor skills and most of his mobility, but his mental facilities never completely returned. He became despondent, suffering emotional and psychological swings that ultimately led to a divorce and a complete separation from his closest friends and family. But he still came to the races, trying to reclaim his past glories as a driver, even though the rest of us knew he could never get behind the wheel of a race car. A "Friends of the Fox" foundation was established for victims of spinal cord injury, and Ron Hemelgarn, Stan's team owner, remains an avid supporter of the foundation's work.

Michelle Marquis gave up driving after the Stan Fox incident, saying, "That's when I realized what the people you care about and those who care about you really go through. I saw the anguish on Lindsay's face as we were waiting outside that hospital. And I knew I could never put my family and friends through that. It was the beginning of the end of my racing career."

Stan didn't die at Indy, but four years later, in the winter of 2000, as he was driving a van in New Zealand, Stan struck another car head-on and was killed instantly. According to published reports, Stan was driving on the wrong side of the road.

From a purely selfish perspective, I find the worst crashes for race car drivers are the ones we can't resolve. If you're bumped or if you get caught in a pileup, if you make a mistake or simply lose it when trying to go fast, you can accept those crashes. You don't like them, and they may frustrate you, but you have a resolution for why you crashed. You know what happened, and that makes all the difference.

It's the head-scratchers, the ones where you don't have the foggiest notion what happened, that get to you. If you stay in racing long enough, you're bound to have one of these incidents, a spinout, or an all-out crash where you have no idea what happened. You think you did everything right; you look at tapes of the crash; you ask around the garage and the pits; and you still don't know. Those are the hardest to swallow. They are also the hardest to erase.

In 1984 I was driving an Aston Martin Nimrod in an IMSA Camel GT race at Road Atlanta, and doing quite well, or so I thought. I was in a rhythm and the car was humming along perfectly. We'd completed sixty-four laps, and I had a scheduled stop after lap sixty-seven, so I was holding my lines before my next stop. There was a right turn at the bottom of the hill, just before the start-finish line. I'd been around it sixty-four times with no problems. I certainly didn't expect any trouble on lap sixty-five.

The next thing I knew I was in the wall. No warning, no reason, no signals or signs, just a full-scale head-scratching crash into the inside dirt bank. After the car was towed in, I spent hours asking people for their opinions on what had happened, but nobody knew. I got a lot of "it could have been"s and "maybe it was"es, but nothing I could hang on to as a legitimate reason for this crash.

Before the night was over it became an obsession. I had to know why I'd hit that wall. I asked mechanics and crew chiefs, track officials and fellow drivers. Nobody could give me a reasonable explanation. Finally, around 9:00 P.M., as I was sitting on the hill staring at the spot where I'd hit the wall, Doc Bundy, the driver who would eventually initiate my fiery crash at Riverside, walked up to where I was sitting.

"Lyn, what are you doing?" he asked.

"I just can't figure out what happened, Doc."

He smiled and shook his head. "Lyn," he said. "There are times when you're never going to figure out what happened. You have to resign yourself to that fact and move on."

I went home that night without an answer. It didn't make me happy, but after a couple of days I realized Doc was right. Sometimes you just have to move on.

PIT STOP

The mind cannot operate on a negative—you can't not think about what's on your mind. If your dominant thoughts are positive, though, they will directly affect your behavior and performance. Learn negative-thought-stopping techniques. Use the Five Rs—Recognize, Refuse, Relax, Reframe, and Resume—which hopefully will work for you.

End of chpt. 9

Deb Turner, Lyn St. James, Trish Moran, and Dick Simon on the
infamous golf cart heading to pit lane.
Photo: Courtesy of William J. Ray/Photos by Ray

CHAPTER TEN

chpt. 10 goes from pg. 183 to 196 (14 pgs)

10

THE GRIND TO BUMP

There was an initial moment of shock when I hit the wall during my 2000 qualifying run; a surreal "did that just happen?" double take from the crew, followed by an audible collective sigh. They had, in a matter of seconds, gone from a euphoric high to one of the lowest lows in racing. In the minute or so following the crash they were both dejected because their hard work and sacrifice had come to this, and at the same time worried about my health and well-being. The crash had been a bad one, and for a couple of minutes, at least, no one was quite sure how I was going to come out of it.

Deb Turner stared at the giant screen behind the front straightaway with her mouth open, not quite believing what she was seeing. The replay was shown over and over again, in slow motion and real time from different angles. Each time the result was the same. The beautiful swamp holly orange car with the distinctive Yellow Freight markings came out of the front straightaway and into Turn One looking great. Everything appeared to be fine through the apex of the turn, then, out of nowhere, the car spun, hitting the inside wall, becoming airborne, then sliding into the outside wall before skidding to a stop. Those were the facts at the moment, and no amount of stunned disbelief would change them. The problem Deb and many others on our crew had was the fact that the big screen didn't show me getting out of the car and walking into the ambulance under my own power. All they saw were continual repeats of the crash.

"Emergency procedure," Trish said to Deb in the pit area.

It took Deb a second to realize what was being said. Then she nodded. We had an emergency procedure for just such an occurrence, with various duties assigned to each team member. According to the plan, Trish was to go to the trackside medical center and keep watch on my progress while Deb waited with a telephone to call my mother.

Everyone knew that John and the mechanics would go to the garage and wait for the car to be towed in. Before releasing the car to the crew, the black box would be removed by track officials who would download and analyze the data while our team studied telemetry readings and videotapes to try to figure out what went wrong. It would be a well-coordinated, if halfhearted, effort. Nobody could be too enthused after what they had just seen on the track.

Dick didn't have time to be involved in any of our post-crash procedures. Twenty-five minutes after I hit the wall, and only five minutes before the final gun of Pole Day, Dick was back in the trough, as Stephan Gregoire sped out of the pit for his third and final qualifying attempt. The warm-up lap was a good one, with Stephan pushing the car over 219 before taking the green flag. This was it. If he didn't qualify the car on this run, he was through.

The first qualifying lap was one of the best Stephan had run all week. As the car sped passed the start-finish line, Richee, who was standing with his dad in the trough, looked at the screen for a number. When lap one was posted as being 219.448 mph, Richee clenched his fist and said, "Yes!" He wasn't ecstatic. There were still three laps to go, and as I had just proven, anything could happen in the blink of an eye, but Stephan was running well. If he maintained this pace, or got a little faster, he could qualify the car.

Minutes later Stephan was in the field with an average speed of 219.970. It was a tenuous speed, but he had made the field for the moment. Any speed under 220 was questionable going into "Bump Day," the second day of qualifying. That was the day when cars that hadn't qualified would make their runs. If a car went faster on Bump Day than the slowest car in the field of thirty-three, then the faster car was in, and the slower car was "bumped." Stephan wasn't the slowest car to have qualified on Pole Day, but he was close enough to the bottom of the list to have a few anxieties going into the second day of qualifying.

Meanwhile, I was sitting on a hard hospital bed at the track-side medical facility. I'd been in this facility many times before. In fact, I'd been only a few feet from this very bed only eight days prior when I came through for my driver physical. A driver gets a pretty good workup before being cleared to drive, including an eye test (a driver's vision has to be at 20/30 or better), blood test, urine check, hearing test, blood pressure and EKG, and a reflex exam.

It was a good medical center, better in fact than most small-town emergency rooms. A low-rise concrete block building located in the infield, the medical center staffed fifteen nurses, six doctors, and a dozen medical technicians in the twenty-bed ER. Most of the time they spent race day treating bee stings, twisted ankles, heatstroke, breathing problems, and alcohol poisoning—normal things you'd expect to see when 450,000 people gather in one place. But the medical staff had to be ready for any and all traumas, including crashes.

All drivers who make contact with the wall are required to go to the medical center, whether or not they think they need it. If the ambulance was dispatched, procedure dictated that you rode to the medical center in the ambulance even if you could jog there. The medical staff then had to give you a thorough going-over before releasing you to drive. It was a good procedure, although it could be, at times, maddening if you were the patient. One year at Indy I broke my wrist in a crash (the most serious injury I've ever sustained in a race car). I knew the wrist was injured from the moment it happened, and when I got in the ambulance I said to the paramedics,

"You guys have any ice for my wrist?" They didn't, and off we drove to the medical center where I repeated my question. "I need ice for my wrist," I said a little more forcefully. "Do you guys have any ice?"

Nobody seemed interested in my wrist. They poked and prodded, X-rayed and EKG'd me to death, but nobody had any ice. Finally, one of the doctors said, "You look to be okay, but you need to go to Methodist for some more X rays." They transported me to Methodist Hospital where I went through even more tests. They X-rayed my legs and took all my vitals before X-raying my wrist. I was still waiting for ice when the doctor came into the emergency room and said, "Everything checks out, but it looks like you have a broken wrist."

Now there was a blinding grasp of the obvious, and I wasn't bashful about letting that poor MD know it. "Of course I've broken my wrist!" I said. "I've only been begging for ice forever."

The Speedway medical personnel were as good as you could find, and Dr. Henry Bock was like the gray-haired hometown doctor everybody wishes they'd had growing up. On Pole Day I sat patiently while they poked and prodded and asked me where I hurt. I couldn't really tell them. As good as they were, a bruised ego and a broken heart were not things they were equipped to deal with.

"I can't believe it, but you appear to be fine," one of the doctors said. "That was a mighty big hit you took out there."

I nodded. I hadn't seen the crash yet, but as soon as I was released I would be heading to the garage. I hoped Dick would be there. I had to find him, not so much to get feedback on what happened, but to tell him how sorry I was. I needed to hear him tell me it was okay. It wouldn't change anything in terms of our current reality, but I still needed to tell him how bad I felt and hear his voice, regardless of what he said.

I knew we didn't have the budget to continue. As far as I knew, my racing was finished. At that moment all I could think about was the crash and whether or not I had done something wrong. I couldn't imagine what I could have done differently. The car had been perfect. I had taken it through that corner exactly the way I wanted, and it had given way without any warning. Surely I hadn't missed something. It couldn't have been my fault, or could it? I had been perfectly attuned to the way the car felt, and it was giving me all the right signals. But sometimes the car lies to you. I needed to talk it through with Dick to make sure this was one of those times.

Roger and Trish were waiting for me outside the medical center when I was finally released.

"Are you okay?" they asked in unison.

"I'm fine," I said. "Where's Dick?"

"We need to call your mother," Trish said. "You really hit hard out there. What did the doctor say? Are you injured any-where?"

"A few bruises, but nothing major. Where's Dick?"

"Let me call Deb. She's standing by to call your mom. You're not dizzy or anything? Did they clear you to drive?"

"Yes . . . no. I mean . . . Where—is—Dick?"

"We'll meet him back at the garage," Roger finally said. "He's just finished up with Stephan."

Ah yes, Stephan. There were, of course, the post-qualifying pictures, interviews, and all the smiling and back-patting that went with qualifying a car for the Indy 500—all the things I would miss this year. I knew Dick well enough to realize he was worried sick about me, but I also knew he would stay out on the line until he answered every last question, posed for every last picture, and heaped mountains of praise on his team and his driver for qualifying. Dick had been at this enough years to master the craft of mental discipline. He was worried about me, but he knew there was nothing he could do that wasn't already being done. His place was in the pits with his other car. Once he finished with Stephan, he would turn his full attention back to me.

We took a golf cart from the medical center to Gasoline Alley. Along the way, concerned Yellow Shirts shouted their support and gave me the thumbs-up as they blew their whistles and moved the crowd aside so we could pass. I heard fans shouting things like, "Glad you're okay, Lyn," and "You'll get 'em next time, Lyn." They meant well, but I wasn't sure there would be a next time.

Back at the garage, I got a lot of hugs and pats, a lot of "glad you're okay"s and "good to see you"s. Deb was there with an update on Mom. Of course, she wanted me to call as soon as possible, which I would do as soon as I talked to Dick.

John was there, and he gave me a huge hug. "I'm so glad we spent all that extra time building the seat," I said. "At the time I was concerned about it. I thought we might be wasting precious time, but . . ."

"I've been around long enough to know better than that," John said. "You can't go fast if you aren't safe in the car. I think today proved that."

It certainly did. I was walking around chatting with the guys in the garage instead of lying on my back in the hospital because of the tedious time and effort John had taken to build my seat correctly and ensure all the safety features were in place. The crash had been unnerving for those who watched it—even Johnny Rutherford said he didn't think it was one anyone could walk away from—but I'm convinced I was fine because of the attention to detail John went through when he fitted me in the car.

A second later I heard the tires of another golf cart squealing outside the garage door. When I peeked around the corner I saw a familiar ear-to-ear smile.

"Dick, I'm so sorry," I said.

He, too, put his arms out and gave me a hug. "Don't you worry, kiddo," he said. "From what I've seen, there was nothing you could do. The rear just let go. I can't explain it. But don't worry about a thing. We're going to get that backup car back. You're going to be in this thing. Just put today behind you, and let's get ready for tomorrow."

Tomorrow? I thought. Bump day was less than twenty-four hours away, and Dick was talking about getting another car ready and up to speed before then. My car was never turning another wheel again, so I didn't know what he was . . .

Then it hit me. He still had a backup car. Dick's third car—the car he wouldn't commit because he wanted to give Wim Eyckmans as much time as possible to put a last-minute deal together—was over in Ron Hemelgarn's garage. Ron had leased the car for Jonathan Byrd's driver, Robby Unser, so he could have a primary and a backup. But the agreement was that if Dick needed the car because of some unforeseen event—like spinning a primary car into the inside wall of Turn One at 220 mph—he could get it back. In our back-to-the-wall effort to get my new G Force built and up to speed before qualifying, I had completely forgotten about the third car. Now Dick was telling me he not only planned to get the car back from Ron, he expected us to tear it down, rebuild it, get it up to speed, and qualify it in less than twenty-four hours. With Dick, that was nothing unusual.

I was dumbfounded, relieved, and exhilarated, all at the same time. I started to prepare myself mentally and physically to be ready to drive on Sunday.

John Martin immediately went to work. "Everybody gather 'round," he said. "Okay, we're getting another car, which means we've got a full night ahead of us. We're going to set it up exactly like we had the primary car before that last lap, which means we've got to change everything. I need everybody to grab a quick bite to eat and get ready. We don't have a lot of time, so let's make every minute count."

The sun had been down for quite some time before Dick got back to the garage with his third car, a G Force with Hemelgarn's Delta Faucet sponsorship logo plastered on the wings and side pods. Robby hadn't had much luck getting the car up to speed in the few practice laps he had turned, so we knew we had our work cut out for us. John had mapped out a plan on the back of a notebook, logging time and manpower requirements for each task that had to be completed between sunset on Saturday and Bump Day on Sunday.

Any other year we would have had a full week between the two qualifying days. In that amount of time we could have bought a new car and spent the time needed to get it ready, run some practice laps, and be confident in what we had before Bump Day. But not this year. We had to squeeze a week's worth of work into about twenty hours. It was a tall order, one I wasn't sure we could fill.

Richee, Justin, and other members of Stephan's crew came over to help. Our garages were side-by-side, but self-contained and separated by a small walkway where the rest rooms were located. It wasn't as though Stephan's crew and the crew working on my car were sharing the same space. Any overlap in effort required members of Stephan's crew to physically leave his garage and come over to mine. I wasn't surprised when, to a man, his crew offered to pitch in and help get my car ready. Stephan had already qualified, so they could afford the time without hurting his program too much. It was a great gesture when they jumped into our garage so enthusiastically.

When I finally got around to turning on my cell phone to call my mom, I noticed I had missed a few calls. As I scrolled through the list, one of the messages caught my eye. Derek Daly, a Formula One, Indy car, and sports car racer who worked in broadcast and was covering the race, had called just a few minutes after my crash. I checked that message first.

"Lyn St. James, this is Derek Daly," I heard Derek's recorded voice say. "I just watched the tape of your crash in slow motion, and I hope you fully understand that this was not your fault. You can see that the tire separated from the wheel as you were coming out of Turn One. There was nothing you could do. Feel free to come by and have a look at the tapes if you want. I know you'll want to see this."

Derek's message was the best medicine I could have received. I would, indeed, look at those tapes—in fact, in the days to come we would study them intently—but for the moment at least I had an explanation that made sense. The car had turned loose too quickly, and the crash had happened much later in the turn than it should have. From what I could remember, I was already opening the steering wheel to set up for the short chute when the spin occurred. A tire separation wouldn't have given me any warning, nor would it have mattered where I was on the track when it happened. If, as Derek had said, the tapes showed the tire separating from the wheel, then I had my answer. It wasn't my fault. There was nothing I could have done once it happened, and nothing any member of the crew could have done to stop it from happening. I left Saturday night feeling a little sore and stiff from the crash, but I also felt relieved. I had crashed, but I had also found a reason for the crash, which added some closure to the day. And as I prepared for the next twenty-four hours, that piece of knowledge proved to be invaluable.

John handed out assignments to all the mechanics with times for each task written out to the side. A suspension change should take four hours; a spring change should take about one. Building the false floor and resetting the pedals should be a two-hour process, and the steering column should take another two. Those duties and a hundred or so others were doled out, along with certain sleeping assignments. With two crews working on one car, John could run shifts. Some of the crew could stretch out and get a couple of hours of sleep while others worked. On paper it looked like we just might pull this off. If everybody stuck to his assignment, we could be rolling in time to qualify this car.

The practical application of the plan turned out to be a little more difficult. If everyone had entered Saturday night rested and ready to work, things might have been different. But the crews had been working twelve- to eighteen-hour days for the past ten days. Couple that with all the emotional pressure of Pole Day, and the guys were simply exhausted.

Men dropped like dead flies throughout the night. At one point, a mechanic was under the car when John heard the unmistakable sound of a wrench hitting concrete. When he bent over to have a look, John saw that the man had fallen asleep underneath the car in mid-turn of a bolt.

He wasn't the only casualty. One of the men lay down on the blanket used to cover the car and fell fast asleep while the pressurized air guns were being used to put the wheels on the car. In the confines of an enclosed garage, those air guns sounded like machine guns at close range. Still, the sleeping mechanic never stirred. John simply grabbed the ends of the blanket and pulled him into an out-of-the-way corner of the garage.

About 5:45 A.M., after having been awake and working for almost twenty-four straight hours, John stepped outside and put his hands on his hips.

"You okay, John?" Steve Melson asked.

"Yeah," John said. "I just have to watch the sun come up. If I see the sunrise, I can catch my second wind. It's like it's just another day."

Steve nodded and went back to work. They still had a lot to do if we planned to get that car in the show on Bump Day.

cht.10

Victory circle at 24 Hours of Daytona.
Jack Roush, Don Hayward (Ford engineer), Bill Elliott,
Lee Morse (holding trophy), Lyn St. James, Tom Gloy.
Photo: Courtesy of Ford Motor Company

CHAPTER ELEVEN

chpt. 11 > goes from pp. 197 to 208 = (12 pgs)

CONTROLLING
YOUR MOMENT

Everyone has defining moments in his or her life and career. Some of the events are small and seemingly insignificant, and some are epic experiences that, in retrospect, make us who we are. The athlete who experiences this moment and those who watch it know they are in the midst of history as it's happening. Lance Armstrong, for example, knew that winning the Tour de France after battling back from testicular cancer was a historic, life-altering moment, and he knew the monumental significance of his victory days before he crossed the finish line in Paris. Kathy Freeman knew what it would mean for her, an Australian Aborigine, to win the Olympic 400-meter race in Sydney, and she knew it before, during, and after the race. That was her defining moment, a night that would change Kathy's life forever.

Most people don't have their lives or jobs played out on an Olympic stage, or in front of a worldwide television audience; so the defining moments are just more private. But certainly no less meaningful. Your friends and family know how important certain moments are in your life, and that's what matters.

There is one big similarity between your moments and the defining moments of the Armstrongs, Freemans, and Lyn St. Jameses of the world. Just like professional athletes, you can control how you live your moment. If you don't, the moment will control you.

I'm not saying you can control everything that happens to you in your life. You can't, and you would go stir-crazy trying. What you can do, however, is control the way you react and respond to the situations in which you find yourself. I remember Lance Armstrong saying that he couldn't control the cancer in his body, but he could control the way he attacked it. He could control the way people saw him as a cancer patient, an athlete, a husband, and a father. They could either see a man who had given up, who had said, "Why me?" or they could see someone who refused to quit, who continued to battle, no matter how insurmountable the odds might seem.

That was Lance's gift to life and to his sport. Before Lance Armstrong, the fan base for cycling in America was smaller than the number of Midwestern families who watched sumo wrestling. After Lance's story of survival, of beating the odds and clawing his way back to the top of his sport, Americans tuned in to the Tour de France with a vengeance. Lance's powerful ascent through the French Alps became a symbol of overcoming the most daunting obstacles, and his charge to the finish became an American metaphor for never giving up.

Like most people, I found Lance's story to be inspirational. Unlike a lot of people, however, I, too, had a somewhat public defining moment ahead of me, and I knew that I would always be remembered for the way I responded to it. Fortunately, I had learned my lesson about controlling my moments many years before I crashed that car on Pole Day at Indy.

In 1987 I was a factory driver for Ford Motor Company driving for Jack Roush of Roush Racing when Ford selected me to be one of the drivers in the historic 24 Hours of Daytona. I felt like I'd won the lottery. At that time in my career, the 24 Hours of Daytona was like the Indy 500. It kicks off Speed Weeks at Daytona and is one of the biggest endurance races in America. To say I was ecstatic would have been an understatement. This was the most thrilling professional moment of my life! To top it off—as if things needed to get better at that point—I learned I would be driving with Tom Gloy, a successful driver, and Bill Elliott, soon to be Winston Cup champion, who had made the cover of *Sports Illustrated* as "Million Dollar Bill." Life for Lyn St. James looked pretty darned good at that point.

As we got closer to race day, my team discovered a minor problem among the drivers. Bill and Tom were tall, lean men with long legs and arms. I'm not exactly short, but compared to those two I was a pygmy. In order for me to fit into the car and reach the pedals after Tom and Bill had driven, I had to insert a "booster" seat. It looked like the kind of thing you would strap a four-year-old into in the back of a Volvo station wagon. But that didn't bother me as long as I got to drive.

I tried to be cool around Bill and Tom, even though I was filled with excitement. Co-driving the car with guys like this would make me a better driver.

We qualified well, and I felt good about our chances. Jack didn't say much, but he never said much. I ignored him, as I always did when he got quiet. There was nothing I could do about his personality, so I just did everything I could to get ready for the race.

The 24 Hours of Daytona is, as the name implies, a twenty-four-hour race. It starts at 3:00 P.M. on a Saturday afternoon and ends at 3:00 the following Sunday. When the checkered flag falls, the car that has turned the most laps is the winner. They also have four different classes of cars on the track at the same time, so in addition to an overall winner, you have winners in each class of car. Obviously, one driver can't drive for twenty-four straight hours, so the race is divided into shifts, with the drivers splitting duty in one car. Sometimes the shifts are an hour; sometimes they're two hours, depending on fuel consumption, tire wear, mechanical repairs, and driver fatigue.

I was scheduled to be the third driver for our team, going out for the 5:00 P.M. to 6:00 P.M. shift. Jack decided we would go out in one-hour shifts first, then gauge how we were doing and adjust the schedule accordingly. That sounded great to me. I stood in the pits with my little booster seat in hand and watched Tom and Bill rack up one great lap time after another. It didn't get much better than this.

At 5:00, when my first shift came, I hopped in the car and sped away with two hours' worth of pent-up enthusiasm. At first I was a little cautious. I couldn't imagine anything more embarrassing than messing up on my first shift after Bill and Tom had done such a great job. After a few laps I couldn't get into a rhythm due to traffic and the fact that the sun was going down, which blinds the driver, but I held my own. When it came time to turn the car over to the next driver, I felt confident that I had done my job for the team. I hopped out, grabbed my booster seat, and went back to the motor home to get a bite to eat before my next shift in the car.

I tried to relax during my first break, but I couldn't. I knew how long this race was and how patient we all had to be. I'd raced in it twice before, and been a crew member a few times as well. Endurance racing has the ability to test everyone on the team. All I wanted to do was go back out to the pits and wait my turn. But I stayed in the motor home, ate a small, balanced meal, and waited, as I should have, for the team manager to call me for my second shift in the car.

Two hours passed, then three with no call. Jack had said he might mix things up a bit after the first one-hour shift, but I had expected to be kept informed of any changes. It would have been nice to know how long I would be waiting before getting behind the wheel, and how long I would be in the car once I got there. I didn't want to make waves, but sending a message didn't seem like too much to ask.

At the four-hour mark, I knew something was wrong.

Even if Jack had extended each driver's time in the car, he wouldn't run more than two-hour shifts this early in the race. Something had to have happened. He must have sent someone to get me, and the messenger had either fallen down or gotten kidnapped between the pits and the motor home. Jack was probably waiting for me, wondering where I was.

With that in mind, I suited up, grabbed my helmet and my seat, and trotted out to the pit where I saw the car running around the track with Scott Pruett behind the wheel. I looked around at Jack and the crew, but no one would look at me. It was as if I weren't standing there waiting to get into the car. Jack had pulled Scott from another one of his cars to replace me as the driver.

"What are we doing?" I asked, trying to be as cool as possible.

Nobody would answer. I was a complete nonentity, an alien standing on the sidelines with a goofy booster seat in my hands. Embarrassed and confused, I went back to the motor home where I waited for someone, anyone, to tell me what was going on.

Another hour passed with no contact. I was miffed now. My second trip down to the pits wasn't quite as cordial as my first. Now Tom was in the car. They had run two shifts without me. I was being blackballed! The biggest race of my career, and I was being ignored like some third-stringer on the sidelines. This wasn't right. I was a driver who had been selected by Ford Motor Company, the chief sponsor of Team Roush, for this race. To be treated like this was humiliating.

I stormed back to the motor home where I paced around for another hour, muttering and swearing to myself. How could they do this to me? It wasn't right, and it wasn't fair. I was a professional race car driver, not some kid begging to get on a carnival ride. This was outrageous behavior, and Jack Roush was at the heart of it. He'd never liked me. He'd never thought women belonged in race cars. He'd . . . he'd . . . Oh!

At 2:00 A.M. I went to a pay phone and called a friend of mine, Don Courtney, who lived in Miami and was a champion race car driver in his own right. The phone rang once when I heard someone pick up and drop the receiver. After a second or two of fumbling, I heard Don mumble something that sounded like "Hello."

"Don, it's Lyn," I said in a low, clipped voice.

"What time is it?"

"It's two A.M. and that's the problem. Don, Jack won't put me back in the car, and I've had it."

"Two A.M."

"Yeah. Now listen, Don. They've blackballed me out of the car and replaced me with Scott Pruett. I drove one shift from five P.M. to six P.M., and that's it. I haven't been back in the car, and nobody in the pits will speak to me or even look at me. I've had it. I refuse to be treated this way."

I got the sense that Don was now semi-awake and paying attention. "What do you plan to do?" he asked.

"I'm quitting," I announced. "I'm calling a press conference where I'm going to announce my retirement from racing, and tell the whole world exactly why. This sport isn't ready to accept a woman no matter how good she is. Well, I'm not going to stand around and be humiliated because of somebody's pigheaded prejudices. I've got too much pride for that. I'll retire and that will be the end of it."

There was a slight pause, then Don said, "Lyn, just relax for a second."

"Relax! I've had it. I'm quitting and I'm spilling the beans on this whole operation."

"Just . . ."

"And I'm going to tell every . . ."

"Just wait . . ."

"Everybody what a complete ass Jack Roush is."

"Just wait a little while, Lyn," Don said. "You can't call a press conference. It's two o'clock in the morning for God's sake. Nobody will come. You can announce your retirement from the roof of the press box if you want, but nobody will write a word. Nobody cares, and you know it."

Now it was my turn to be silent.

"Look, I know you're upset, and rightfully so. Even if there is some legitimate reason for Jack to keep you out of the car, he should at least tell you what it is. But you can't control that. No matter how hard you try or how much you want to, you can't control what someone else does. The only thing you can control is how you react and what you do. Things aren't going your way, but the answer is not to quit. If you do that, they win."

I sighed, then said, "I know, but it's just not fair. It's not right."

"No, it's not, but that has nothing to do with you," Don

said. "Look, why are you in this race in the first place? Why do you drive race cars?"

"Because I love it," I said.

"Exactly," Don said. "Why would you give up what you love because of some odd duck like Jack Roush?"

I chuckled for the first time. Don was right. I couldn't quit this sport, and even if I did, nobody would care.

"Look, when they want you to drive, go drive. Until then, get some sleep."

That's exactly what I did. After thanking Don for putting up with my ranting and for offering such great advice, I stretched out on the bed in the motor home and fell asleep for almost three hours. Nobody called me to drive in that time, so I slept great. When I woke up at 5:30 I was rested and ready. If Jack wanted me to drive, I would be the freshest driver on the track. By then I knew Jack didn't want me to drive, so I decided to give him a little encouragement.

The rest of the people at the track looked like zombies. By 5:30, the race was well into its fourteenth hour and all the cheers of excitement and enthusiasm that had been present when the green flag fell on Saturday afternoon had been replaced by blank stares and inaudible grunts. After three hours of shut-eye I was the best-looking person there.

I found Lee Morse, the Ford representative, who had just arrived back at the track after spending a restful night at his hotel, at around 5:35 A.M. "Lee," I said without preamble. "Jack hasn't put me in the car since six P.M. yesterday, and I have no idea why. I'm a Ford factory driver. You're paying me to be here, and I'm doing nothing but eating and sleeping. Plus, I've only driven one shift. If I don't get four hours in the car, I won't get any points or be listed as an official driver."

The points issue was a big part of my strategy. A driver had to spend at least four hours in the car to receive points for this race. This was the first race of the season, so if I could earn points at this race I had a shot of going for a championship for Ford Motor Company. If I left the 24 Hours of Daytona with no points, it killed my chances of being the point leader at the end of the year. So Ford Motor Company had a vested interest in seeing that I spend at least four hours in the car.

Lee called a meeting with Jack and me, which took place next to the pit box with cars screaming by us.

"Lyn says she's being kept out of the car, and she doesn't know why," Lee said to Jack. There was no small talk at this hour of the day.

Jack shrugged. "The clutch is broken in the car," he said. Then he turned to me. "Can you shift gears without a clutch?"

"I've never done it," I admitted.

"We were going to put you in this morning. You don't do as well at night, and we're leading the race, so we were going to wait and use you after the sun came up. But now the clutch is broken, and I can't jeopardize our lead if you've never driven a race car without a clutch."

He had me. If I persisted, it would look like I was putting my own selfish interests above the team's position in the race. As for the "driving at night" issue, Jack made it look like he was being the brilliant team owner, utilizing his drivers for

207

RIDE OF YOUR LIFE   207

maximum efficiency, but since I hadn't even driven at night I don't know where he came up with that.

Then an idea hit me. "Okay, Jack," I said. "You've got a pretty comfortable lead at this point. Put me in the car at the next change. If I can't change gears without the clutch, I'll immediately bring it back in, turn it over to another driver, and spend the rest of the race cheerleading from the pits. You won't hear another peep out of me. But if I can shift without a clutch, and it doesn't jeopardize the integrity of our lead, I'm driving the car."

Lee was nodding before I finished. "That sounds reasonable to me," he said.

There was nothing Jack could say. At the next pit stop, I put on my helmet, strapped myself into my booster seat, and sped out of the pits.

To his credit, Jack patiently talked me through the shifting procedure. You can't force a shift change when you don't have a clutch. You can easily grind the gears and ruin the transmission. You have to time it perfectly, quickly moving from one gear to the next as the engine hits a certain number of rpms. It takes a little adjustment and finesse, but after a couple of shifts, I got it. Jack asked me to leave my radio open so he could hear the shift changes. After a couple of changes, I heard him say, "Good . . . good job."

I drove for almost three hours on Sunday morning without ever missing a beat or a gear. My lap times were good, and we maintained our lead, but in the middle of my third hour, the seat belts began cutting into my left leg. The dang booster seat had perched me forward in such a way that the belts were strapped over my thighs instead of my torso. After a while circulation became an issue. I radioed that I needed to be relieved, and I came in on the next lap.

After a massage and some fluids, I went back out for my third shift, running one more hour in the middle of the day. That gave me more than enough time to qualify for points. I was, in the eyes of track officials and our team, an official driver at the 24 Hours of Daytona.

We won our class and finished seventh overall. On Sunday afternoon I was standing on the podium holding the 24 Hours of Daytona trophy with Bill Elliott and Tom Gloy at my side. It was my biggest racing accomplishment to date. And to think that twelve hours before I had been ready to call a press conference and quit racing because my feelings were hurt. What a lesson! What a night!

PIT STOP

It is not the events in our lives that determine the outcome, it is our perception of those events. You have 100 percent control of what you believe, so you can change the outcome by your thoughts and actions. If you believe in yourself and motivate others to believe in you, there is nothing you can't achieve.

CHAPTER TWELVE

Chpt. 12 - goes fm 209 to 230 (22 pgs.)

MAKING THE SHOW

12

When the track went green at 10:00 A.M. on Bump Day, Sunday, May 21, 2000, we still had all four wheels and a couple of the A arms off my car. It had been a long night, and the crew looked like a group of battle-weary soldiers. Nerves were frayed, and everybody was on edge. No one lost their cool—we didn't have any all-out fights in the garage—but the tension was thick, and conversations were clipped and to the point. Time was running out and everyone knew it.

John remained steady and calm, even though fatigue was beginning to show. His eyes sagged a little, and the deep, bass voice cracked a couple of times as he was directing traffic in the garage. The crew had done a remarkable job. I knew they were exhausted, but I also knew they wouldn't quit until the job was done. Indy crews take great pride in their work. When a car goes fast, it's a reflection on them. This crew was no different. They wanted this car in the Show as badly as I wanted to be driving it.

The temperature on Sunday hadn't warmed up much. I could still see my breath when I arrived at the track, and by 10:00 A.M. the air temperature was only 56 degrees under cloudy skies, and the track was a chilly 74 degrees. That worked to our advantage in one respect: we had a cold-track setup from the day before that we knew was good for at least 221 mph. But different cars respond differently to the same setup, so we needed to get out on the track as quickly as possible. If all the stars aligned and every variable worked in our favor, the setup on the car we had crashed Saturday afternoon would work perfectly on the backup car we would take out on Sunday afternoon. But that was a lot of wishful thinking, and John, Dick, Steve, and I all knew it. We needed to turn some laps, and we needed to do it soon.

When I first arrived at the track on Sunday morning, I walked quickly and smoothly through the garage and put my hands on my hips as if I had just come back from a morning workout at the gym. I needed to send a signal to everyone that I was okay, even though I was sore from my hair to my toenails. Nobody would see me move slowly or step gingerly. I felt a few twinges of pain immediately after the crash, but the adrenaline surge on Saturday kept me from feeling the full effects. The seat and safety features had kept me from jostling around and breaking any bones, but pulling those kinds of g-loads takes a toll on your body, and by Sunday

The team after qualifying for 2000 Indy 500.
Photo: Courtesy of William J. Ray/Photos by Ray

morning I hurt in places where I didn't think I had nerve endings.

Fortunately I was no more banged or bruised than I had been in some of my other crashes. Soreness was something you lived with in our sport, and I knew that when the time came to drive I wouldn't feel a thing. Focus makes you forget the little aches and pains, and this was a day when I needed more focus than I'd ever mustered as a race car driver. Sitting in the garage watching the team work on the car, I felt like I'd been tackled by the entire front line of the Tennessee Titans, but once I got in the car, I knew I could push the pain away.

Bump Day was our last chance. I wasn't going to let a few bruises stand in the way of our goals.

⬜⬜

The track opened at 10:00 A.M., and a flurry of cars sped onto the track. Pole Day had been exciting, but Bump Day was an entirely different experience. This was desperation time for many teams, and "let's make a deal" time for many drivers. There were a lot of cars in the garage area that hadn't been qualified—either backup cars or cars that weren't ready in time for Pole Day—and a lot of drivers trolling Gasoline Alley trying to put together last-minute deals in the hopes of getting a ride. At times it looked like a Turkish bazaar with deals being struck in the rest room corridors and contracts being signed on top of tires. It was now or never for many drivers, and a lot of team owners were willing to take smaller sponsorship deals on Bump Day because the alternative was to have their car sitting in the garage during the race.

Unlike most auto races, you qualify the *car* at the Indy 500, not the driver. One driver can qualify another car, but then he or she has to be removed from the original qualified car and that original car goes to the back of the field. Some team owners, like Eddie Cheever, choose to keep a backup car handy in case something happens to his primary car. Others shop their nonqualified cars to the highest bidder. Bump Day is one of those days where the bidding intensifies as owners and drivers vie for one last chance at making the Show.

Bump Day is also a day of great anxiety. After all thirty-three cars have qualified, the slowest car in the field is said to be on the "bubble." Any car that runs faster than the time posted by that slowest qualifier is in the race, and the slowest car in the field is "bumped." Once a car is bumped it cannot attempt to qualify again. So if a driver only has one car, and that car is perched on the bubble, the feelings of helplessness and anxiety can become overwhelming.

After having raced in six consecutive Indy 500s, I was bumped from the field in 1997 and 1998, and I felt like crawling in a hole. There's nothing you can do. You're standing in pit lane watching the board and calculating the lap times, but the end result is out of your control. If you're in the thirty-third spot, the next car on the track could bump you out of the field and send you home. It's a cutthroat, high-stakes, zero-sum game where one team's victory is another team's loss.

At the beginning of the day on Sunday, only twenty-three cars had qualified. That left room for ten more cars to make the Show before bumping would begin. This time I was the one trying to earn my way in at the last minute. If I had to bump someone else out of the field, so be it.

Before we could even think about qualifying, we had to get on the track, and that was proving to be a cumbersome and time-consuming task. Robby Unser's setup on the car was diametrically opposed to the setup we wanted. We had to change everything. By 10:00 A.M., we weren't even close. The springs were in place, the false floor had been built, and the pedals and steering column had been moved. We were close on the suspension, but close didn't cut it on Bump Day. Progress seemed to creep as the clock continued to tick. We still had a couple of hours of work before we could turn our first lap, and I was becoming more than a little concerned.

Billy Boat, coming off a frustrating Pole Day where he had to wave off his first qualifying attempt and didn't even take the green flag his second time out, was the first on the track Sunday morning. His crew had worked late into the night getting the car ready, and Billy drove it well. He posted one lap over 219 mph in the first fifteen minutes of practice, then quickly jumped up over the 220 mark, running a practice lap of 220.227 before bringing the car back in for tech inspection.

The track appeared to be fast, and there was no shortage of nervous drivers near the bubble who wanted things to slow down before noon.

Bump Day qualifying started a little later than Pole Day proceedings because of a military ceremony at the track. Sunday was Armed Services Day, and the George family had always gone out of their way to honor America's fighting men and women. Bump Day was no exception. At 11:15 the ground shook as an F-16 fighter squadron from the 122nd Fighter Wing performed a low-altitude flyover. That was followed by a parachute drop featuring the Golden Knights, the Army's elite jump team out of Fort Bragg, North Carolina. Dick took a couple of minutes away from the garage to watch the jumpers, and I followed him out of the garage.

"How are we doing?" I asked as the Golden Knights jumped out of the aft end of a C130.

"We're getting there," Dick said. I expected that response, but I just wanted to hear him say it, to hear the timbre of his voice. I had learned to gauge Dick by his inflection as much as by the words he used. This time I could tell he was tired, but he believed we would make it. And if Dick believed it, then I believed it, too.

When the jumpers opened their chutes, red, white, and blue smoke began streaming from canisters on their boots. They crisscrossed paths in the sky, slowly floating back to earth with precision accuracy. It was a beautiful exhibition.

"We didn't have those when I was jumping," Dick said. "I used to strap flares to my boots and have them burning while I was free-falling, but nothing like that. Man, those flares were hot. I don't think the manufacturer intended for them to be used that way."

"Probably not, Dick," I said. And we ventured back into our garage to check on the progress.

Two minutes after official qualifying began, Raul Boesel
entered the field with a four-lap average speed of 222.113, a
benchmark that sent gasps through the grandstands. The
track was running fast. Anybody who expected to maneuver
into the field today had better be ready to post some good
numbers.

Billy Boat went out immediately after Boesel, but Billy
didn't fare as well. After a warm-up lap that barely nudged
past 217 mph, he got a little faster, turning in a lap of 217.992
mph. Then he pushed a little too hard, and the car spun into
the wall in Turn One. It wasn't a huge crash—Billy climbed
out of the car before the emergency team arrived—but it did a
fair amount of damage to the left side of his car, and it
knocked Billy out of the morning qualifying session. His only
hope was to get the car fixed or get into another car before the
final gun at 6:00 P.M.

Billy's crash prompted a string of bad luck. Minutes after
the track went green again, Johnny Unser was forced to wave
off before completing his first lap. Davey Hamilton couldn't
get up to speed either, and waved off on his first lap. Jacques
Lazier, the rookie brother of former Indy 500 winner Buddy
Lazier, aborted his run on his warm-up lap after the car lost
power, but eleven minutes later, at 12:44, Jacques was back out
on the track. This time he qualified his car with speeds of
221.762; 221.152; 220.248; and 219.544 for a four-lap average
of 220.675. Another rookie would race in his first Indy 500.

I would have been happy for Jacques had I not been so preoccupied with getting our car on the track. We finally had everything in place. Dick, John, Steve, and Richee were going over the numbers one final time before we took the car out.

I changed into my race suit in the ladies' room next to the garage. Trish, the NASA engineer who had been the calming force in the moments following my crash, still acted as my personal attaché, carrying my gloves and helmet and running interference when the crowds became too overwhelming. The fans were wonderful, yelling their support and offering their best wishes throughout the day, but sometimes it got to be too much. I had another qualifying run to make, and it was important that I be able to prepare myself both mentally and physically for the hours that lay ahead. Trish understood that, and went to great lengths to make sure I had a zone of privacy.

Once dressed, I walked back to the garage with my race face on. The last of the Yellow Freight decals were being applied, and although the car wasn't as artistically appealing as the one I had crashed on Saturday, it was all we had. If it ran over 220 mph and qualified for the race, I would view it as the most beautiful car I'd ever seen.

"We've got the same setup she had in the last lap yesterday," John told Dick.

"No rear wicker?" Dick asked.

"No rear wicker, and no wing angle. We've got a three-sixteenth wicker on the left front and one-eighth on the right front. Cold tire pressures are thirty-one on the left and thirty-six and thirty-seven on the right."

Dick nodded. It didn't look the same, but the car was as close as we could get to an exact replica of the one I'd spun into the wall twenty hours before.

"Okay," Dick said. "Let's get it out and see how it does."

The track went green at 2:00 P.M. after no cars were presented to qualify. Toward the end of the front straightaway, before the entrance to Turn One, stands a huge black pole with lighted numbers running from top to bottom to indicate the cars that have qualified and the speeds they have run. When we took the track for the first time at 2:07 P.M., there were still eight blank spots at the bottom of the pole. The 2000 Indy 500 had room for eight more cars. After that, it was the dog-eat-dog world of bumping. Either way, I was ready. If the car got up to speed quickly, I wouldn't hesitate to take it out before we had a full field. If we didn't have the speed, we would wait and take our chances.

"Kiddo, your track temp is a hundred and ten degrees," Dick said. "Let's go out and get a system check and put a little heat on the tires."

I gave him the thumbs-up, then listened as the starter fired the engine and the crew pushed me out of the pit box. Running through the gears on the warm-up lap, I had already managed to clear my mind of everything that had happened on Saturday. It was a new day and a new race car, so I started with a clean slate. I didn't have time to think about anything but getting this car up to speed. The gun was going off in less than four hours with or without us. There was no time for flashbacks.

I brought the car in after one complete lap and we down-loaded the data and did a systems check. At 2:15 I went back out and attempted to get in my first lap at speed in the new car. The car felt loose in all four turns, and I brought it back in after getting it up to only 208 mph. There was no reason to keep a bad car on the track any longer than necessary. We needed to make adjustments quickly and get back out.

"How about a one-eighth wicker on the back?" Steve said.

"That's exactly what I was thinking," John said. The two of them had worked together as a team on this car without a hint of ego. They had relied on each other, called on each other, and worked hand in hand during some of the most demand-ing circumstances in racing. No matter how today turned out, these two men deserved all the credit in the world for what they had accomplished.

"Lyn, we're giving you a little more downforce," John said.

"Tire temp's thirty-seven on the left, front and rear, and forty-six on the right front and rear," I heard Dick say.

"She should be all right with that," John said.

Dick nodded and stepped back, standing in front of the car to eyeball the wing angles. This had become a ritual, and I felt comfortable being back in a routine I had seen many times before.

"Track's pretty open," I heard the Turn-One spotter say.

"All clear back here," Sara said from Turn Three. She was back on her perch, watching traffic coming out of Turn Two and down the back straightaway. Like everybody else, Sara sounded a little tired, but I was glad to have her out there.

"Let's go," Steve said. And the crew pushed me out of the pit box again.

This time the car pushed in every turn. The looseness had been corrected, but we overdid it considerably.

"Yellow flag, yellow flag," I heard Sara call, but I had already seen the lights flashing on my dash. In addition to flashing lights around the perimeter of the track, each car's dash system also flashes yellow whenever there's a problem on the track.

"Coming in," I said.

"Roger, Lyn, you've got a yellow flag. Copy you coming in."

This time the yellow flag was simply a signal that a car had been presented for qualifying. When that happened, the yellow flag came out, the Speedway staff spent a couple of minutes inspecting the track, and the qualifier was given the signal to proceed.

Jimmy Kite qualified his G Force with an average speed of 220.718, becoming the twenty-sixth qualifier on the board. Ten minutes later, Davey Hamilton put a car on the board with an average speed of 219.878.

Time was running out on us, but that was part of the chess game team owners played on Bump Day. Those who were already in the Show could stretch out the afternoon by putting cars in line that they had no intention of qualifying. If they presented a car, the track would automatically go yellow for inspection. That cut down on the number of practice laps others could run. Some owners also put cars in line they had no intention of even running through tech inspection. They simply lined the cars up to make the queue appear longer. Long lines and short time windows tended to suck cars into the qualifying queue before they were ready. Experienced crews knew how many cars could get on the track in a certain amount of time. If the number in line exceeded the number that could qualify before the gun, your car had better be sitting in line waiting, even if you knew some of the cars ahead of you were going to pull out. It was a stall tactic, a mind game employed by those already in the race to keep others from bumping their way into the field.

But we still had six cars to go to reach a full thirty-three-car field. I thought it was a little early for such tactics, but I was one of the ones trying to earn a spot in the field. If I'd been on the bubble, I probably would have wanted all the delays I could get.

Dick and John had done this long enough to know when we needed to be in line, and I had to trust them when it came to the timing of our run. I couldn't bog myself down with things I couldn't control. I needed to be in the car when we were ready to run, so I made the decision to stay in the car until we either qualified or ran out of time. Normally when the car is on pit lane, or when it's being hauled back to Gasoline Alley for fuel or a fresh check on the scales, the driver gets out of the car, stretches, gets a drink, or maybe makes a quick trip to the rest room. I chose to do none of that. My place was in the car, and that's where I would stay.

Robby had struggled with this car. He'd never gotten the car above 207, and he was on his last attempt with his primary car. No matter how fast this car ran, if he took the green flag, that was it. I was a little surprised when I saw his first-lap speed at only 214.092. He could fill a spot with that speed, but not for long. Unfortunately for Robby, things got worse from there. His second lap was 213.716, his third was 213.008, and his final lap was 209.952 for a qualifying average of 212.678. He was in the twenty-eighth spot, but that speed would never hold.

After Robby returned to the pits, the track opened up again for practice. We needed to get a few more laps in as quickly as possible to dial the car in before putting it in line. No cars were being presented at 3:45, but I knew that by 4:45 the queue would be filled. Whatever we were going to do to the car, we had better do it in a hurry.

I couldn't see much from the cockpit, but I could sense the worry around me. Trish was standing next to the car holding an umbrella over my head to keep the sun off of me, and I could see a strained expression on her face, as well as a more frantic pace from my crew. Tensions were mounting. We needed to post some fast times, and we needed to do it quickly.

Just as we were getting ready to go out, Stan Wattles hit the outside wall in the short chute between Turns One and Two. The car did a quarter spin and came to rest on the warm-up lane at the entrance to Turn Two. Stan was fine. He, too, got out of the car on his own power before the ambulance arrived, but his crash sent the yellow flag flying again. Every one of these delays narrowed our time window. We had to get out there and get some laps in before putting the car in line.

The track didn't go green again until 4:02, minutes before I knew the line would begin to fill. Once again, the moment we were ready to go out, another yellow flag dropped. This time Hideshi Matsuda, the only Japanese driver attempting to qualify, did a half spin and slid into the outside wall at the entry to Turn Three. Hideshi also got out of the car on his own, but he was moving slowly. A couple of minutes later Tom Carnegie announced that Hideshi had been transported to Methodist Hospital for X rays of his right arm.

We finally got out on the track at 4:27, where I immediately hit the rev limiter in fourth gear. The car was still pushy. We were running out of time, and I didn't have a car I could qualify!

"Yellow flag," I heard after my second lap. Another car had been presented. It was looking more and more like our best efforts at qualifying for this Indy 500 would all be for naught.

Johnny Unser qualified at 4:37 with a speed of 219.066. The track was getting slower as the day dragged on, but we still didn't have a full field. Less than ninety minutes before the final gun, only twenty-nine cars were qualified.

"Look, I want us to go minus seven clicks on the front wing and minus two flats on the ride height," Dick said. "We'll use a one-sixteenth wicker. Got it?"

Everybody nodded. No one was in the mood for small talk. I focused on my view from the cockpit, going through the visualization exercises I'd learned over the years, playing and replaying my most positive experiences from this Speedway, breathing deeply, sharpening my focus on the track, blocking out all the outside distractions. The guys at Human Performance International had helped me hone the mental skills required for this type of waiting. When the time finally came for us to qualify, I would be ready.

At 4:45 we went back out for what I knew would be our final practice run. If we didn't get it right this time, we were done. The new setup felt better, but I could tell we didn't have the speed we'd had the day before. The good news was we didn't need it. We weren't going for the pole. Anything in the 219- to 220-range should be good enough.

My first lap I turned at 208.914, but I could tell the car was getting faster. The turns felt better and I was able to hold my lines with more confidence. A second lap showed 217.391. That was close. One more lap, and I should . . .

"Yellow flag, yellow flag," I heard over the radio.

"What now?" I said to myself. It turns out Donnie Beechler had run out of fuel, and the track went yellow while his car was towed back into the pits. By the time I got back to our pit box, Andy Hillenburg was in line to qualify. That was it. We were through running laps. It was time to either qualify the car or go home. We'd done all we could do in the time that we had. Now it was time to line up.

While we were back in Gasoline Alley putting methanol in the car with me still sitting in the cockpit, Andy put his car in the Show with a speed of 218.285. It wasn't the fastest car on the board, but he wasn't on the bubble, either. By the time Andy got into the pits and accepted the congratulatory pats from his crew, we were in line. Happy Hour was under way, and, as predicted, the place was a madhouse.

At 5:02, when Scott Harrington went out for another attempt, Robby Unser was pacing up and down pit row. He knew he had the slowest car on the board, and if any bumping took place, he would be out of a ride. It was a sinking feeling. I knew, because I'd been there. Robby was a grown man from a racing family, and he knew what this day was all about. The final hour of Bump Day could be the cruelest sixty minutes in motor sports. But it could also be the most glorious.

At 5:05 Doug Didero raced out onto the track. From the beginning Doug's car didn't look right. A driver can sense when a car isn't taking the turns the way it should, and Doug's car was definitely having trouble. When he came around Turn Four and headed down the front straightaway for his warm-up lap, I wondered if he would wave off before taking the green flag.

He never got that chance. Doug's car spun in the apex of Turn One and slid into the outside wall, sending his left rear wheel and most of the suspension pieces flying into the fence separating the track from the grandstands. The car then did another three-quarter spin through the short chute before stopping on the warm-up lane at the entrance to Turn Two. Doug climbed from the car without assistance, but the groans in pit row were palpable, even over the sounds of the engines.

"Damn," Dick said. He wasn't prone to swearing, so on the rare occasions when he did say something off-color you stood up and took notice. "This is going to push everything back. How many cars ahead?"

"Looks like four ahead of us," Steve said.

The Speedway crew was already out on the track, clearing Doug's car and putting down oil dry where the crash occurred.

"Sara, how much oil dry is going down?" Dick asked Sara Senske, who was still at her station in Turn Three.

"It's hard to tell from here," Sara said.

"Well, you need to tell," Dick shouted. "I've got to know whether or not to send Lyn out on the track and what the conditions are going to be. Look at the spots where they've put down the oil dry and gauge how much is on the track. Is there enough to cause any slipping?"

Dick was right on the edge now, and everybody on the team could see it.

After a long pause, I heard Sara say, "She should be okay. I'll stay up here for one more run just to make sure, but she should be okay."

That next run didn't come until 5:18 when Billy Boat, fresh out of the garage with a new suspension after his earlier crash, stalled three times before finally getting his car out of the pits and onto the track. When he took the green flag, it was obvious the car still had problems. The first lap was 217.412, and Billy squeezed out a good second lap with a speed of 219.085. But that was all the car had in it. The third lap was 150.928, as the engine seemed to lose compression. The final lap was 198.724 for a four-lap average of 192.105. Billy was in as the thirty-first qualifier, but he was the new man on the bubble. The first car to qualify once bumping began would boot Billy right out of the field.

"Oil dry looks fine," Sara said. "I'm coming down."

"Roger that, Sara," Steve said. Whether or not we qualified the car, Sara wanted to be in the pits to see it, and to be there for me. This was a once-in-a-lifetime opportunity for her to witness the best efforts of men and women who had faced impossible odds. I wanted her in the pits, in the arena, almost as much as she wanted to be there herself.

Steve Knapp qualified the Team Purex car with an average speed of 220.290. That made thirty-two. The next car to qualify would fill the field. I was two cars back. If I were getting into the Show, I would have to bump somebody out. From the looks of things, Billy Boat was the most likely candidate.

The line through tech inspection was even more of a circus than it had been on Pole Day. When Sara arrived I saw Juan Montoya, a CART driver making his Indy debut, make a beeline for her. As I was sitting in the car waiting for the line to move, Juan propped his foot on one of my tires and started flirting with Sara. Now this suave Latin rookie was hitting on my protégé while Dick was scurrying around the car checking tire temps and wing angles. If the weekend could get any more surreal I didn't want to know how. I was two cars away from my last chance at Indy. I sat in the car as it went through the tech line. If anything else happened—if one of the cars ahead of me in line crashed and sent the track yellow again—I wasn't sure I'd have time to make a run. Jack Miller, a practicing dentist whose mother is his primary sponsor, filled the field of thirty-three with an average speed of 216.154. All remaining entries would bump other drivers out of the Show.

I was next out. As I pulled into the stall, Brian Barnhart greeted me as he did every driver, every time: "When I give you the signal, exit the pit lane and go directly onto the race-track. You will get one warm-up lap, then be sure your crew waves either the green or yellow flag. If there is a green flag or no flag, the starter will give you the green and it will be considered a qualifying attempt. Good luck!"

"Fire it up!" John shouted to the crew. Gary Green grabbed the starter and moved behind me. A second later the engine roared to life.

As I pulled down pit lane I remember saying, "God, it's in your hands now. We've done all we can do. But please don't do to me what you did yesterday. If we're meant to qualify this car, so be it. If we aren't, then there's nothing more we can do."

"Go! Go! Go!" Steve shouted.

Now I was ten miles from glory. What a long, strange trip it had been.

Gary Green was checking the telemetry in the pits when I came out of Turn Four and headed into my official warm-up lap. "She's going flat!" Gary yelled to the crew. I had put the pedal to the floor and cruised through Turn One without a hint of a lift. I had to get everything the car would give me.

"It's a good one," Dick said from his usual spot in the flag station. My warm-up lap was 214.286, not as fast as Pole Day, but good enough. "Go get 'em, kid!" he shouted as I passed.

Lap one was 219.566 and I knew the car had more. I never lifted and never took my eyes off the track. The lines were right in front of me. I could see them. I could see them before I reached them, and I could feel the car responding to my

input. My confidence grew with each turn. This wasn't the car
I had on Pole Day because we had 20 gallons of fuel, anticipat-
ing we'd get one more practice run before qualifying, but it
was a car I could drive into the Show, and that was all that
mattered.

The second lap was better than the first. When I turned in
a 219.618, Sara Senske raised both arms and screamed "Yeah!"
She wasn't alone. Gary and the crew were shouting and leaning, craning their necks to see my every move through Turn
One. When I hit the back straightaway, I could sense that the
car wasn't quite as fast as it had been on the first two laps, but
it still seemed fast enough. I was in the zone. "Just feel the car,
Lyn," I said to myself. "Sweet, smooth, perfect lines." My third
lap was only 218.664. I couldn't get anything more on the last
lap. I was flat-footed all the way around and took the fastest
lines I could find through the turns. It still wasn't as fast as I'd
gone in my first two laps. Lap four was 217.670.

"I'm sorry," I said over the radio to whoever would listen.
I knew I'd missed it. There was no way those last two laps had
bumped me into the field. When I rounded Turn Four and
headed down pit lane and finally saw the board, I couldn't
believe it. The number 90 glowed on that long black pole like
the North Star. I was in. I'd bumped Billy Boat. I was in the
Indy 500.

As I drove down pit lane, past the pit boxes where the
other teams were either frantically working to get their cars
onto the track or breaking down and getting ready for the rest
of the week, I saw a gauntlet of people lining the edge of the
lane. Mechanics, crew chiefs, team owners, drivers, and friends

from every team lined up to congratulate me as I passed. I felt pats on my helmet and I saw thumbs-up signals from people three and four deep in the crowd. We'd done it. In the last moments of the last day of qualifying we had pulled off a feat like nothing I'd ever experienced in my quarter century of racing.

When I stopped the car, took off my helmet, and crawled out of the tub, my team was there, haggard, exhausted, spent, and smiling like the happiest people on earth. In that moment, with everything we had accomplished staring back at me in the smiling faces of my teammates, I sat on the left front tire of the G Force we had just qualified, and I wept without shame.

CHAPTER THIRTEEN

chpt. 13 goes from pg. 231 to 240 - 10 pgs

THE GLORY OF
TEAMWORK

13

Moments after I qualified the car for the 2000 Indy 500, Speedway officials hustled me into the media center, where I sat at a large table on an elevated stage and spoke into a microphone about what it meant to be in the Show for a seventh time. It was tough to rein in my emotions, but I did manage to string a few cohesive sentences together.

"These last couple of years I went through times I would not want anyone to go through," I said. "I know what it's like to be on the board and get bumped. The last two years of not making it into the Show really tore me up inside. This was the strongest test I've ever had in knowing who Lyn St. James really is. Yesterday's crash was a big hit. It put a big dent in our program, but I have to thank Dick Simon and the whole team for what they did. The team worked twenty-four hours in shifts to put the new car together, and it jelled. It worked! Our motto has always been, 'Yes, we can.' Now we've done it, and it feels fantastic."

It would have been nice if I could have brought the entire crew in for that interview, because this qualifying run belonged to them as much as it belonged to me. Having a team pull together like ours did during that single weekend in May was the experience of a lifetime. Fortunately I was able to drive the car fast enough to earn a berth in the Show, but my efforts would have meant nothing if my team hadn't pulled the all-nighter. If Dick Simon had come in after my crash on Saturday and said, "Well, it was a good try. We've lost our chance, so I think we need to pack it in," we would have been through. If John Martin had said, "It can't be done. We can't get another car ready in time," we would have all been watching from the grandstands on Sunday rather than celebrating in the pits. If our crew had said, "The heck with this, we're out of here," we couldn't have pulled it off. Without the full commitment of every single person on the Dick Simon Racing Team we wouldn't have made it, and I wouldn't have been sitting behind a microphone answering questions.

"The car was wonderful on the first lap," I said. "That helped my confidence. As for how this experience ranks in my career, I'd say it ranks really, really high. In fact, I'm still driving that last lap. I'm still looking at the board for the number ninety car. This is just a great day for our entire team."

I couldn't mention the team enough. The job they did and

The joy of victory. The crowd cheers our finish at my
first Indy 500 in 1992. Photo used with permission of the
Indianapolis Motor Speedway Corporation.

the efforts they put forth were phenomenal. Working with a team like that made the qualifying victory even sweeter.

On the other side of that same coin, I knew what it was like to have a rift within a racing team, and I had learned from past experience about the value and the glory of teamwork.

In 1985, after being named Rookie of the Year for the IMSA Grand Touring (GT) series the previous year, I finally persuaded Ford Motor Company executives to sponsor me for ten GT races in the 1985 season. I drove a Mustang for Roush Racing that year, and the team dominated all year. As the season progressed I had goals of winning the series championship by accumulating the most points for the year. But as far as the team was concerned, if anybody from Roush Racing was going to win the championship that year it was going to be one of my teammates, Johnny Jones or Wally Dallenbach, Jr. I was simply an add-on who brought more funding from Ford Motor Company.

Tensions within my team were palpable throughout that year. The team manager, Charlie Selix, considered me an ancillary part of the program, and I never felt like part of the team.

The most glaring example of my status within the team occurred in September of 1985 at the Serengeti 500, a 500-kilometer Camel GT race in Watkins Glen, New York. I was coming off a victory at the Elkhart Lake race in August along with my co-driver Johnny Jones. That victory moved me into the top five in points for the year. Everyone was asking me if I felt we were going to win at Watkins Glen since we'd just come off the win at Elkhart Lake, the theory being that wins often come in bunches. I'm not sure I believed that, but it sounded good to me. I was feeling confident.

Watkins Glen was one of my favorite tracks. Our car was running well, and I felt comfortable with the track. It was going to be a long race, but September in New York was the perfect time of year to go fast.

In GT endurance races, two or more drivers are required to be listed on the entry. At various intervals in the race we changed drivers. In April of that year, I'd driven our Mustang into the lead at Charlotte Motor Speedway only to watch my co-driver Bruce Jenner (yes, the Olympic decathlon champion) crash on his first lap behind the wheel. Just like that we were out of the race, and there was nothing I could do about it. I'd been in enough endurance events to know that it's just part of racing. Plus, I'd made my share of mistakes over the years. But this was only my fifth year as a factory driver for Ford Motor Company, and I was on a mission to demonstrate to them that I was a winning driver. With so much on the line at Watkins Glen, I didn't want anything to go wrong.

Whitney Ganz was my co-driver, a replacement for Bruce Jenner, who wasn't able to make this race. I knew Whitney, and knew he was a very good driver, but he wasn't that familiar with our car.

In the early going, I built a substantial lead over the field. We definitely had the fastest car that day, and I was in the zone, seeing the track and the other cars, and visualizing my turns better than I had in a long time. It was a crisp fall afternoon, and I felt great behind the wheel. I wasn't tired, hot, or in any way out of sorts when it came time for our scheduled pit stop.

When it came time to make our pit stop for fuel, tires, and the driver change, I was not ready to give up the car. I wasn't tired, and I wasn't hot. We were leading, and I was in a good rhythm. Getting out of the car at that point didn't make sense to me. I don't think it would have mattered who was there to drive—I just didn't want to put anyone else in the car. There were too many variables I couldn't control, and it was a risk I wasn't willing to take.

I stopped in the pits with my five-point safety harness drawn tightly around my body. During a normal driver change a driver loosens the belts while driving down pit lane. That makes it easier for the new driver to strap in quickly. But I had no intention of going anywhere other than back out onto the track. When I stopped the car in the pit, I didn't move.

Whitney was standing there ready to help me out of the car, just as we had practiced. I didn't respond. He tried to release the netting that fits where the window is so I could crawl out, but I shook my head and kept my hands planted firmly on the wheel. I'd made my decision. I wasn't getting out of the car.

With new tires and a full load of fuel, I sped out of the pit and back onto the track, leaving Whitney and the rest of my team standing in the pits with quizzical looks on their faces. I never consciously pondered the ramifications of what I had done, before or after that pit stop. I just did it. I do remember thinking for a moment that if I didn't win this race I may as well not come back. I could just turn left out of the track and head to the Elmira Airport. My relationship with the team wasn't the best in the world, but I was hoping that a win today would improve things. I certainly wasn't trying to slight Whitney, but I needed to be in control of my own destiny. This was a big race for me, and I wasn't going to leave my fate in anybody else's hands.

I won the race by a healthy margin, and on the victory lap I dropped the netting and waved to the cheering crowd. We had won, so we all should be celebrating.

But we weren't all celebrating. I drove the car into the victory circle, got out amid a throng of media and well-wishers, and was promptly escorted to the podium. It was late in the day, and the sun was setting on the trees behind the track. The crisp air tasted and smelled wonderful from my perch atop the winners' podium. It was a moment I should have shared with the rest of my team, but my team was nowhere in sight.

The trophy presentation came, and I held the hardware high for the crowd to see, but not a single solitary soul from my team joined me on the podium. The other class winners were surrounded by their teammates—co-drivers, crew chiefs, owners, and mechanics all found room on the podium for pictures and a congratulatory group hug—but my team was nowhere around.

After the trophy presentation and victory pictures, I tried to believe the best. Maybe they had gotten tied up at the garage. Maybe they were all waiting for me back in the garage with a bottle of champagne. Maybe this slight wasn't as I was taking it. When I got back to the garage, I realized that it wasn't as I was taking it; it was much worse. The crew was gone. The car had been loaded onto the truck and the team had gotten into their cars and driven away without so much as a good-bye, good job, or good riddance. They had simply left.

I was personally devastated. Okay, maybe I should have given the car up, but at the time I didn't think that was the right call. I won the race. What did it take to get these guys to believe in me? I left the track feeling hurt and confused. The victory was hollow because, in the end, the team wasn't there to share it with me. As a side note, that victory at Watkins Glen ended up putting me in the record books as the only woman driver to win a GT race driving solo. I just wish I could have shared the pride of that accomplishment with the team.

Later that season I was still in the points chase going into the season-ending race at Daytona. Because of budget cut-backs, the decision was made to run only one car with three drivers for the finale, and I was one of the three. During the race Charlie Selix pulled me out of the car so I didn't earn any points toward the championship. This was the final race of the season, and I didn't earn any points for the win. I didn't find out until that evening at the awards ceremony. Johnny ended up winning the series that year, and I finished third in the points.

I learned a lot about myself from that season, and I learned about the importance of having the grace to handle victories and defeats the same way and the value of team-building and what it can mean to your future. We all must rely on help from others at varying points in our lives and careers. Developing solid relationships based on trust and mutual respect is the best way to reach your goals and build the kind of support that will help you in the long run. You can't do it alone; you need to build your successes with a solid team of people who believe in you.

In 1994 I had a team experience that drove that lesson home. JC Penney was still our sponsor that year, but only for the Indy 500. While I was disappointed that we were only going to do the 500, I also knew that it meant we could focus all our efforts and resources on the most important race of the season. We were able to put together a new chassis, fresh engines, and the best crew with plenty of time to prepare for what could be my best Indy 500. The downside was that anything can happen in a one-race season. A crash, a failure to qualify for whatever reason, and we wouldn't simply be done for the week or the month; we would be finished for the year.

I remember fretting about that prospect for the first couple of months of the year until Dick and I talked and he put together a great team that included Emory Donaldson, who had never been to Indy but had started with me in the Pinto days and was a top-notch crew chief; Tony Vondongen, who had been with me for my two previous Indy 500s; and Dane Hart, a bright, young mechanic eager to prove himself. We

had the freshest, brightest, most cohesive unit in Gasoline
Alley that year. The crew worked well together and were
behind me 100 percent. They didn't leave a stone unturned.
The car was good, but no better than the fifty or so other cars
attempting to qualify that year. It was our team that made the
difference. The group acted as a single unit with no single
hero and no one lagging behind.

I qualified sixth in 1994, the best starting spot in my Indy
career, and outqualified a couple of world champions: Mario
Andretti and Nigel Mansell.

The value of teamwork cannot be overstated, and the
glory of sharing success with those who helped you get there
is one of the most rewarding experiences you'll ever have.

PIT STOP

*People want to help others achieve their goals. Reach out
for help, build a strong team, and share your success. Focus
on helping others attain their goals as you reach yours, and
there's no limit to how much you can achieve.*

CHAPTER FOURTEEN

Chpt. 14 > goes from pp. 241 to 260 = (20 pgs)

LADIES AND GENTLEMEN

By the end of Bump Day, it dawned on the reporters that for the first time in history, two women had qualified for the Indy 500. Before I left the media center I found myself answering questions about Sarah Fisher and what it meant to have two women racing against each other in the Show.

"I just wanted to be in the race," I said, a little put out at that stage by all the gender questions. Sure, Sarah and I were women, but we were also accomplished race car drivers, among the thirty-three best that year, anyway. I was certainly proud of Sarah, but I wanted to move past the gender issue, and so did she. If we couldn't drive, we wouldn't be there, regardless of our sex.

I was tickled to death that two women had qualified for the race, but I thought that focusing solely on our gender detracted

14

from our racing. Sarah and I were race car drivers who happened to be women. As long as we were viewed in that context I didn't mind talking about our accomplishments. Sure, we were women, and sure, we were the youngest and oldest drivers in the field, but we had also put substantial speeds on the board in order to be where we were. I tried to make that point in all my remarks to the press.

Everyone from the Yellow Shirts, to fans, to other mechanics, to my fellow drivers made a pilgrimage to our garage to say "Great job." It was a rewarding moment, and one I didn't mind celebrating. We had a week before the race, and the car wouldn't go out on the track again until Carb Day, the following Thursday. In the meantime, everything about the car would be changed. The setup, the suspension, the engine, the ride height, the springs, the bars, and just about everything else would be new and different for the race. But we had a day or so before we had to think about those things. Right now, it was nice to enjoy the moment.

I had plenty of media appearances lined up on Monday, including an ABC shoot at 9:00 P.M. that night. But after qualifying in such a dramatic fashion, the requests quadrupled overnight. My knees and legs remained a little sore after the crash, but the rest of my body rebounded better than I had expected. By race day I would be completely healthy and pain-free.

We all have times when we wish we could be in two places at once, and this was certainly one of mine. The team had been through so much together. I felt I needed to be with

During the race, Sarah Fisher in Car #15 behind me coming out of Turn Four before the crash in Turn One. Photo used with permission of the Indianapolis Motor Speedway Corporation.

them, especially given the fact that Wednesday was Community Day, a sort of Speedway open house where fans of all ages could walk through Gasoline Alley and meet their favorite drivers. Lindsay was graduating from high school in Vail, Colorado, on Wednesday and I wanted to be there for her. So I had had to ask special permission from the Speedway management to miss the mandatory events of Community Day, but Brian Barnhart had been more than kind in letting me go. "Of course," he had said. "You should be at your daughter's graduation."

That's exactly what the fans said as well. Deb put on quite a display in our garage, stuffing a race suit with pillows and foam and sitting it in a chair outside our garage door with a sign out front explaining why I wasn't in it. "Good for her," fans said throughout the day. "That's exactly where she needs to be."

I flew to Vail on the Laziers' Lear 35 with 1996 Indy 500 winner Buddy Lazier and his dad, Bob. When we arrived at the Eagle Airport, I drove to Vail and met Lindsay at the beauty salon where she was getting her hair done for the pregraduation prom. When I saw the look in her eyes as I walked through the door, I knew I'd made the right decision. Some things were more important than racing. This was one of them.

The ceremonies went well. Lindsay attended Vail Mountain School, a private school with a small graduating class, so the exercises were more intimate than those held at larger schools. The headmaster called each graduate to the stage and gave a personal anecdote about each student. Then he asked the parents to join him onstage to present the student with his or her diploma. It was a nice touch, and one I was glad I was there to experience.

The only uncomfortable moment came when the headmaster mentioned me in his comments about Lindsay. "For those of you who don't know," he said, "Lindsay's mother, Lyn St. James, just returned from Indianapolis, and she'll be going back immediately following this ceremony. Lyn has qualified and will be racing in the Indianapolis 500 on Sunday."

I was embarrassed for Lindsay. The headmaster was kind, and he meant well in mentioning me in that way, but this was Lindsay's moment. None of the other parents were recognized for what they did. There were surgeons and scientists in the room, people who did far more important things than drive race cars for a living. But I was the one singled out, because I was the famous Indy car driver. It was awkward, and I later apologized to Lindsay.

"It's okay," she said, but I knew she felt a tinge of disappointment. "I'm just glad you could be here."

I was glad, too, even though I had to leave shortly after the ceremony. I had to get back to Indy for Carb Day on Thursday morning. Missing Community Day could be excused, but I had to get back to work. I rented a car and drove to the Rifle, Colorado, airport where I had leased a King Air 300, a twin-engine turboprop, to carry me back to Indy on Wednesday night.

At 3:00 A.M. on Thursday, I walked through the charter terminal at the Indianapolis International Airport and asked the leasing agent who I needed to see about paying for the plane. "It's already taken care of," he said.

"That's impossible," I said. "I just leased this King Air at the last minute to fly back from Vail, Colorado."

"Yes, ma'am," he said. "Someone named ... let's see ... someone named Dick Simon called and took care of it. He said to tell you congratulations, and he hoped the graduation went well."

I stood there speechless for a moment.

"Ma'am, is everything okay?" the attendant asked.

"Yes," I said. "Everything's wonderful."

I arrived at the track early on Thursday morning with my race face on for Carb Day. We had spent an enormous amount of effort getting the car set up for qualifying, but the race day car had to be completely different. In qualifying you're on the track alone. There's no traffic to maneuver in and out of, and there's no drag from other cars to disrupt the wind flow over and under the car. The car is set up for smooth aerodynamic performance. You also qualify with about 10 gallons of methanol in the tank, just enough to get in four good laps. On race day you carry a full 35-gallon load, with each gallon weighing a fraction less than seven pounds. That added weight not only changes the balance of the car but also shifts the flex points and alters the ride height and aerodynamics. Then there was the engine. Qualifying engines are built differently for qualifying, so you want a fresh, race-prepped engine for the race. A fresh engine can run about 600 miles at over 10,000 rpms. The race is 500 miles, so you're pushing it if you get in too many practice laps on Thursday and then try to run the race. To attempt to race with the same engine you had in the car for qualifying is not the best plan, but we were about to do it. I'd crashed the car with my qualifying engine in it, so the engine we used on Bump Day was the one I would have to use during the race. Fortunately, we had put only 57.5 miles on the engine during our Sunday qualifying session. The engine should hold through the race. When you put all those pieces together, the car you take out on Thursday doesn't come close to resembling the car you qualified the previous weekend. Unfortunately in our case, most of the changes were for the worse.

"Carb Day" is short for Carburetor Day, a throwback name dating to the days when Indy cars had carburetors and mechanics spent the Thursday before the race tuning them. It's also the last practice session before race day, a final chance for teams to dial in their race setups before the green flag falls on Sunday.

We were a long way from having a setup we could race, and we were running out of miles and time to dial it in. Every lap you ran on Carb Day was one less lap the engine had for race day. You could certainly spend the full two hours on the track on Thursday if you wanted. You could run fifty or sixty laps and get the car tuned exactly the way you wanted it. But what would you do on Sunday when the engine broke with forty laps remaining in the race? I always believe that the fewer laps you put on the car on Carb Day, the more laps you had on race day. That was especially true this year. We already had some hard miles on that engine from our Bump Day qualifying session. Every lap we turned on Carb Day was a risky one. Unfortunately, we had to turn more laps than we wanted on Thursday, because we were grasping at straws.

"I've trimmed the right front wicker and given you five clicks on the front wing," John said after I posted an abysmal lap of 200.758 mph.

"Whatever we need to do, let's do it quickly," I said. "We're running out of laps."

The changes didn't work. The fastest lap I could post was just under 204 mph, and the car pushed through every turn. We had nothing, but we were out of time. The new engine had 84.5 miles by 1:10 in the afternoon. That was close to our limit. Any more laps and we ran the risk of blowing the engine during the race.

"Let's take it in," Dick said. "We'll make a couple of changes in the garage and get it dialed in."

Always the optimist, Dick assumed we could find the magic formula with the car sitting on the scales in the garage. I hoped he was right, but I knew from the tone of his voice that it was wishful thinking.

I left the track on Thursday concerned about our prospects but happy to be racing. We'd overcome so much to be in the race I somehow knew things would work out for the best no matter what the outcome. On Thursday evening two syndicated DJs, Bob Kevoian and Tom Griswold, of the "Bob and

Tom Show," held a back-row party for the three drivers in the thirty-first, thirty-second, and thirty-third spots in the field. The Speedway held a formal gala for the three drivers in the front row—the pole sitter and the second and third qualifiers—so these two guys started their back-row party as part spoof, part good-time-rock-and-roll Thursday night bash. Because I was in the back row, I attended the party with Dick and Dianne Simon and thanked everyone for their support.

The weekend of the race was like old times. It had been three years since I'd been in the race, which meant I'd missed the drivers' meetings and the parades, and I hadn't hosted my annual pre-race dinner on Saturday night. But now things were back to normal. I was once again sitting in the bleachers for the drivers' meeting, and I once again got my ring. I rode on top of one of the pace cars during the parade and waved to fans lining the streets of downtown Indianapolis as they sent their cheers of support to me.

Because my apartment was also downtown, I walked home from the parade route. Along the way fans stopped me and congratulated me on my qualifying run. Some even shouted from rooftops as I passed by. "Go get 'em, Lyn. We love you," they yelled. I waved and smiled and tried to keep my cool. This was pretty heady stuff given what I'd been through in the Month of May.

Later Saturday night I held my traditional small dinner party for my closest friends and a few sponsors, a quiet gathering downtown on the canal in the National Historic Society building. Since my rookie year I had learned that an intimate gathering the night before the race actually gave me energy rather than sapping it out of me, the way some of the more elaborate functions did. Another source of energy, relaxation, and preparation the night before the race was a massage, so I excused myself early for that important treatment.

Before I woke up the next morning, a small city within a city descended on the Speedway as 450,000 people made their way to the track from all points on the globe. The gates opened at 5:00 A.M., and a mass of humanity swarmed inside. By the time the green flag fell, the Indianapolis Motor Speedway would become the second largest city in the state of Indiana.

I arranged for a police escort at 6:30 A.M. on race day so I didn't have to worry about the miles of cars lining the streets in every direction. We sped right into the entrance of the Brickyard Resort, and I parked behind the motor coach and walked to the garage as I had done almost every day for the past two weeks. Deb and Trish were already there, having spent the night in the motor coach finishing last-minute details. But today was different. Electricity filled the air. People were more alive and alert than at any other time during the month. This was what the Month of May had led to, what we had all worked for, and why we had come to Indianapolis in the first place. It was time to race in the most prestigious motor sport event in history, and the largest spectator-sporting event in the world.

Then it was time to get suited up and make an appearance at Dick's hospitality tent. Yellow Freight had invited 200 guests and customers, and they were expecting me to appear for a pre-race speech. They told me it was the first time that they had had 100 percent response and attendance for such an event.

I spoke about how hard our team had worked all month and how ready we were to put on a great race. It was the "Yes You Can" Yellow Freight car No. 90 they would be watching on the track.

Then it was "quiet time" for Lyn St. James. I was amazed at how quiet the garage area got on race day. The crew and car were out on the track, access to the garage was limited, and everyone seemed to move at a more relaxed pace.

Tony Robbins, the author and motivational speaker, had arrived at the track on Saturday, the day before the race, and volunteered to give the whole team a pep talk. So the entire Dick Simon Racing Team gathered in the media center at 3:00 P.M. to have a personal presentation from Tony. Considering he charges a fortune and speaks to hundreds of thousands of people all over the world, it was quite an honor to have him at the front of the room in the media center with about forty members of our team. Tony appeared nervous at first, which fascinated me, and made me realize even the best get nervous.

It didn't take long for him to get rolling. At one point Tony said, "Dick Simon lives motivation, the rest of us talk about motivation." Tony focused on how each of us sends a message of confidence and "readiness" just by our physical stature, posture, and facial expression. He asked me to try to display my state of mind when I crashed in qualifying, and then to display my state of mind when I successfully qualified and was in the zone. When you are thinking about anything else other than the action of whatever you are doing, you cannot be in the zone. He had all of us stand up and take partners and do some physical exercises to demonstrate our personal power. It was fascinating and quite inspiring.

To my surprise Tony showed up in my garage area about 10:00 A.M. on race morning for a one-on-one pep talk. I had been a fan for quite some time, and felt privileged to have this opportunity. Tony helped me get to another place in my mind by asking me when I'd had my best finish at Indy.

"My rookie year," I said. "I finished eleventh."

"Well," he said, "if you managed to have your best finish when you had never raced in the Indy 500, then there is no reason you shouldn't be able to have a great performance today, especially since this is your seventh Indy 500."

Tony turned my mind around and had me focus on the positive. He also said some pretty nice things about what I'd accomplished over the years, so I must say my confidence level was boosted. As he left he said, "I'll see you after the race!"

Even a little rain couldn't dampen the charged atmosphere. The race was scheduled to start at 11:00 A.M., but a sprinkle around 10:30 postponed things a little. Once the rain stopped about 12:40, Brian Barnhart, the IRL director of operations, announced that the race would start between 1:45 and 2:00 P.M. if no more rain fell. Giant blowers attached to tow trucks swept the track and sped up the process. Before long, we were in the cars and on pit lane. All we needed was the call from Mari Hulman George, chairman of the board, to start our engines.

At 2:01 P.M., after Florence Henderson sang her rendition of "America the Beautiful" and Jim Nabors belted out a verse of "Back Home in Indiana," Mari stood on the podium at the winner's circle and said words that had never before been uttered at the Indianapolis 500.

"Ladies and gentlemen," she said. "Start . . . your . . . engines!"

The traditional pronouncement had always been, "Gentlemen, start your engines," until Janet Guthrie and I came along. Tony Hulman (Mari's father) couldn't bear to say "Lady and gentlemen," so the first year Janet raced the words were, "In the presence of a lady, gentlemen, start your engines." Rumor has it that because the cars are not started by the drivers but by a mechanic outside of the cockpit, he was technically correct. I've always said I really didn't care what they said. When it was time to go I was going. Now with Sarah and me in the same race, the command to start engines for the Indy 500 would be "Ladies and gentlemen"—that was how it should be.

If only my car was how it should be. The changes we made on Thursday hadn't worked, and in the first ten laps of the race I knew I was driving a sled. My straightaway speeds were between 210 and 215 mph, and cars were passing me like I was backing up. It was all I could do to hang on or get out of the way. Drivers could go around me at will. High, low, any turn they wanted, they were speeding past me.

"We've got a serious push everywhere," I called in over the radio.

"Yeah, we see that, Lyn," John said. "Next stop we'll add a little more wing and see if we can't get you a little closer."

"Let's do it in a hurry," I said.

My first pit stop came at lap thirty-three after I'd averaged 206 mph on my previous four laps. "This thing's all over the track," I told the crew. "I've got a lot of push at entry, but it doesn't want to stick on exit, either."

"Let's go up six clicks on the front wing," John said. "That should take care of the push."

"I hope so," I said.

The crew changed all four tires, fueled the car, and made the wing adjustments in less than twelve seconds. Unfortunately, the car still wasn't up to speed. I fumbled around at 207 mph for another twenty laps before pitting again. We were losing ground at an alarming rate.

"We need to do something here even if it's wrong," I said.

"Going with a one-eighth wicker on the rear, plus three more clicks on the front," John said.

Fifteen seconds later I was back out.

The weather front that had created the rain earlier had finally blown through, but in its wake there were some pretty good wind gusts through Turn Two. Certain spots on the track became like wind tunnels with whatever breeze was in the area channeling down the track like a funnel. When you hit one of those gusts going over 200 mph, you knew it. The car was getting slower by the second, and there didn't seem to be anything we could do about it except get out of the way.

The first yellow flag of the race came out on lap sixty-six when Greg Ray got caught in a wind gust and slid into the outside wall at the exit of Turn Two. Al Unser, Jr., also hit the wall after making contact with several flying parts from Greg's car. Both appeared to be out of the race, and we proceeded under caution for six laps.

When the track went green again on lap seventy-one I did everything I could to stay out of the way. My car was slow and everybody knew it, so I did the courteous thing and took my corners high, giving drivers plenty of room underneath me.

Three laps later, just before entering Turn One, I checked my mirror and saw a blue car a couple of car lengths behind me. The next moment I saw its nose on my left. The driver was trying to pass underneath me. No words from the spotter, but I couldn't help thinking, "Wow, that's an aggressive move."

An instant later, I was into the outside wall of Turn One. The car making the aggressive pass had clipped my left side and pushed my car up into the wall. But the blue car hadn't fared any better. When I came to a stop I saw that it, too, had made contact with the wall in the short chute between Turns One and Two.

Then my heart sank. The other car belonged to Sarah Fisher. Both the "ladies" Mari had been speaking to in her introduction had crashed together in Turn One. We were both out of the race.

What kind of fate was this? What sort of odd quirk of luck would bring the two female drivers together in one fateful crash? I had spent the previous day and the days before that, and the decades before that, doing everything in my power to have women drivers viewed as simply drivers, but the questions had continued to come. "What sort of historical significance do you think having two women in this year's race will have?" one had asked. "As a woman, what sort of advice would you give to Sarah?" came another. Nobody asked me what sort of advice I would give Juan Montoya, another Indy rookie. The only reason Sarah and I were the focus of so much media attention was because we were women. Now we had crashed together, and I knew the press was going to have a field day.

At the moment I had a few questions of my own. What on earth, I wondered, would cause Sarah to try to make such a high-risk pass this early in the race?

I never saw the third car, but John Martin did. From his vantage point in the pits John saw Jacques Lazier trailing Sarah down the front straightaway, and he could sense what was about to happen. Jacques had been on Sarah's tail for three or more laps, and from the gyrations he was making with the car, Jacques appeared to be growing tired of the view. From John's vantage point, it looked like Jacques had made up his mind to pass Sarah in Turn One, and nothing was going to change that plan, even the fact that my car was already there.

John knew what was about to happen, but there was nothing he could do about it. He'd been there before himself. As he liked to tell it, "Years ago in Milwaukee I was racing against Dick Simon and did the exact same thing as Jacques. I'd followed Dick for about twenty laps and I'd had enough of it, so I decided that I was going to pass him in Turn Three or eat it trying. Dick lifted a little early, so I dove for the bottom and made my move. What I didn't know was the reason Dick had lifted. A car had spun out and was sitting on the track facing backwards right where I had decided to pass. The driver was actually getting out of his car, so I thought, 'Man, I'm going to cut him in half.' I made one quick move to the outside, but I cut his car and my car in half. I got airborne and spun three hundred and sixty degrees before coming down and sliding to a stop all the way into the front straightaway. It wasn't till I stopped that I knew the whole right side of my car was gone. It was pretty bad, but it could have been a lot worse, all because I got impatient and told myself I was passing Dick right then or else."

That was exactly what Jacques had done. He made up his mind he was passing Sarah in Turn One, and the fact that there were three cars trying to go through Turn One at the same time never occurred to him. Sarah had moved up trying to avoid Jacques. I was already there, so Sarah hit me. The cruel irony of the whole thing was that Jacques, the driver who caused the crash by making a rookie mistake, was the only one who didn't crash. He slid through unscathed and finished thirteenth in the race.

Montoya, the rookie Indy 500 driver who had propped his foot on the wheel of my car while flirting with Sara Senske on Bump Day, won the race in convincing fashion, pulling away from Buddy Lazier in the final laps. I saw the finish from the garage. Dr. Bock gave me a quick going-over and determined that the only thing hurt in this crash was my pride.

"Those bruises from the other day seem to be healing nicely," he said.

"Yeah," I said. "I just wish I didn't have to be here again. I mean, I love you, Dr. Bock, but . . ."

He laughed. "I know. I'm not the most popular guy to visit on race day."

I thanked him for everything he'd done. As I opened the door exiting the medical center I was greeted by a horde of television cameras and reporters asking me what had happened. I was the veteran. I was the one they wanted to talk to. Plus, as I found out later, Sarah hadn't checked into the medical center, so the reporters were waiting to hear from me. To make matters worse, I still didn't know about the third car. I gave my honest, but limited, view of the incident and got back to our garage. I just couldn't believe our race was over, and that we had crashed a car again.

John was right. It was certainly bad luck, and it wouldn't stop the press from having a field day, but gender had nothing to do with why we had crashed. Three cars had tried to go where only two would fit. The driver who caused it had gotten away with it, and Sarah and I were left to lick our wounds and ponder all the things that might have been.

I've never gotten caught up in the feminist aspects of what I did for a living other than to acknowledge that there are plenty of great women drivers in the world who will eventually break through and compete at the highest level. I always

chpt.14

Tony George accepting helmet from Lyn St. James after last
laps at Indianapolis Motor Speedway.
Photo by Emmanuel Lupe of Dick Simon Racing.

260.

wanted to be known for going fast, not for bei
driver." It was a shame that the only run Sarah
have together at Indy ended the way it did. But I w
left the track that day having been treated fairly by
and the media who covered the event.

Three drivers entered Turn One at the same tin
only one came out. It's happened countless times bei
Indy, and will no doubt happen again in the future.

And gender has nothing to do with it.

CHAPTER FIFTEEN

LAST LAPS/NEXT LAPS

A year after that fateful Sunday crash I was back in Gasoline Alley listening to the sounds I'd heard a thousand times before. But everything was different in May of 2001, and I found myself drinking in the atmosphere with fresh eyes and ears. There were the whistles from the Yellow Shirts and the squeals from the golf carts, all the noises I'd grown to love over the years. And there were the fans who leaned over the railings and pressed against the fences to shout words of encouragement.

At that moment I knew I was going to miss this track more than I had originally thought.

Emotionally and intellectually this was the toughest decision I'd ever made, but it was the only logical choice I had. I was fifty-four years old, a young fifty-four, but the calendar didn't lie. I was surrounded by twenty- and thirty-somethings in a sport where the slightest slowdown in reaction time meant a hell of a lot more than just winning or losing. I'd been the oldest Indy 500 rookie at age forty-five, and having younger male drivers around me was never intimidating, but the wisdom born from having lived through more birthdays than most other drivers could carry me only so far, and I knew it. It had been a full year since I'd driven an Indy car, and it had been a half dozen years since I'd competed in a season that extended beyond the Indy 500. No matter how experienced you are as a driver, one race a year isn't enough to keep your wits sharp and your skills honed. Perhaps I could have qualified for the race, but it wouldn't have been the same. I would have been hanging on, and I respected the craft of race car driving too much for that. If I couldn't compete to win—if I couldn't be at my best—then I knew it was time to retire from Indy racing.

May 6, 2001, would be my last official day driving an Indy car. I might run a few test laps in the future, but as far as prepping a car for race day, this would be it. There were plenty of other things I wanted to do with my life, among them continuing to develop young drivers through my driver development program. I would continue to serve on the board of Kettering University, one of the top engineering schools in the country, as well as other philanthropic boards working on behalf of women's sports and cancer education and research. And I would continue to race. I'd already been invited to race at the Goodwood Revival in England in the fall of 2001, so I knew I wouldn't be far from my passion. But Indy racing would be behind me.

I would be the first driver out on opening day, and if everything went as planned, I would take a few laps around the old Brickyard one more time. Then I would stop on the historic yard of bricks. Reporters and photographers would be waiting, or so I hoped, and assuming I ran my laps without any problems, I would get out of the car and present my helmet to Speedway president Tony George. My run would be a ceremonial display, something I wasn't completely comfortable with, but it was better than sending out a press release and quietly disappearing.

I felt I owed it to the fans to take these last few laps. For ten years these people had been the most loyal, enthusiastic fans I'd seen in any sport. From the moment I took my first competitive turn around this track in 1992, men, women, boys, and especially little girls lined up twenty-, thirty-, sometimes forty-deep to get my autograph, shake my hand, take a picture, or simply wish me well. Today was no exception. As I rode out to pit row in the front seat of a golf cart, hundreds of fans lined the fence outside Gasoline Alley shouting things like "We'll miss you, Lyn," and "Give 'em hell, Lyn. Go out in style." Any reservations I had about this little display disappeared at that point. I owed these people one final show, and I planned to give it all I had. They deserved it. I wouldn't retire as a winner of the Indy 500, but I would go out in style.

The idea had originated two weeks before in Atlanta. The Indy Racing League had a night race at the Atlanta Motor Speedway a week after I had made my decision to retire, and I wanted to share the news with the other drivers, owners, mechanics, and crew chiefs. I couldn't imagine anything worse than having my friends, including Dick Simon, learn of my retirement in the newspaper. A phone call wouldn't do, either. I'd known these people too long. The only way to do it was face-to-face, and that meant traveling to Atlanta.

When I arrived in the garage area at the Atlanta Motor Speedway, the crews were working as they always did, frantically fine-tuning their cars for a few practice runs before Saturday night's race. Drivers rode BMX bikes back and forth between the garage and the pits, and support staff scrambled to keep plenty of food and water in the paddocks. I, on the other hand, felt queasy. As I headed out to pit lane I found myself avoiding conversation with old friends for fear that I might have to admit I was hanging up my helmet. Even though I had come to Atlanta for that very purpose, the reality of announcing my retirement made me ill. I quickly exited the pits and headed for the rest room, where I threw up. At that moment it dawned on me that this might not be the best way to put my Indy career behind me.

That's when Emmanuel Lupe stepped in. "So, how are you planning to announce your retirement?" he asked in his silky French accent.

"I don't know," I said. "I came here to tell some friends, but I guess I need to put together a press release or something.

I can't tell everybody, and I don't want to answer questions about why I'm not in a car for the next four weeks."

"No, no," Emmanuel said, waving his arms with great flair. "We must stage an event. Dick is taking an extra car to Indy. Why don't you drive it on opening day? You can be first on the track, take a few laps, then present your helmet to someone from the Speedway. I will coordinate a press event around it so you can answer all the questions at once."

I gave Emmanuel a huge hug. Getting back in an Indy car, even if it was only for a few warm-up laps, was an opportunity I couldn't turn down. But I tried to contain myself. Dick had a race to run at Indy, and another driver to consider.

"Do you think Dick will mind?" I asked.

"I will ask him, but . . . pffffh." Emmanuel waved his hand and pursed his lips as if to suggest such thinking was absurd. "If you still have your license and we can coordinate it with the Speedway, it should be no problem." In the first couple of minutes of thinking it through, Emmanuel's idea didn't appear to have a downside.

I renewed my license and checked with the Speedway officials to get everything cleared. Of course, I didn't consider my emotional response. When the time finally came, as I was riding out onto the line in my race suit, a decade of feelings welled up inside me. One little girl behind the barricade yelled, "We're going to miss you, Lyn," as I passed by, and I almost lost it. I shook my head and cleared my emotions. I was about to crawl into the tub of one of the most demanding race cars on earth, and there was no room for emotions once I got behind the wheel. This was certainly not the time or place to get weepy, especially since some local reporters were giving two-to-one odds that I would cry.

When I got to pit lane Dick was there, pacing like a nervous coach before kickoff. He hadn't aged a bit in the previous year since we'd last been together on this track. He was just as bald and his smile was just as big. He still looked like he would blend in better at an actuarial convention than at a racetrack, but there was still no one on earth like him.

In the past year, Dick had been in another remarkable incident. He'd been racing a Cigarette boat in the International Grand Prix off the coast of Florida, pushing his aquatic machine over 90 mph when he heard a crack and felt the rear of the boat come around. The driveshaft had broken. The boat was out of control. It flipped twice, end-over-end, throwing his throttle man clear. But Dick's leg was pinned between the bulkhead and the console. As the boat flipped, this sixty-seven-year-old was slapped twice against the bulkhead like a rag doll. The boat came to rest upside down in the water but was sinking fast. Even with a broken leg and cracked ribs, Dick scrambled out, waving to the passing helicopter to signal that he was fine.

"I didn't want them to have to send in the divers," Dick said. "By the time I got out from under the boat they were already in the water. I really felt bad, but I just couldn't get out any faster."

Now he was walking around the pits without a trace of a limp or a hint of a scar. He was as amazing as ever.

"We could use a little less front wing," Dick said to Richee after inspecting the car I was about to take out.

I just smiled. He would tinker till the day he died, and I loved him for it.

"So, are you ready for ziss?" a husky French voice asked from behind me.

I turned around and saw an old friend, Gilbert Lage, giving me a knowing smile. Gilbert had worked with Dick for years, but was now on Sarah Fisher's crew. He understood these pre-run rituals as well as anyone. The two of us leaned back against the concrete wall on pit row and watched as Dick and Richee scurried around the car making adjustments.

"Hell no, I'm not ready for this," I said. "I know I can still drive. I just can't go around the country chasing money for the rest of my life. I'll continue to race something, just not Indy cars."

"I think they're ready for you," Gilbert said, nodding toward Dick.

I glanced at Gilbert's watch and saw that it was almost 1:00 P.M. The track opened at 1:15, and I wanted to be the first driver out.

I walked over to the G Force—the sleek, aerodynamic missile of a car with open wheels—and stepped into the tub while inserting my earplugs and pulling the balaclava over my head. I buckled the helmet into place after I slid my butt into my seat and found the familiar pedals with my feet. Everything fit perfectly, just as I remembered it.

The view out of the cockpit was also familiar. There was

Dick, running back and forth between his two cars, and Richee, checking the radios, measuring the wicker on the rear wing, and confirming fuel levels. Gary Green was in the pit as well, locking my steering wheel into place before hauling the starter over the pit wall.

Just like old times, but with one noteworthy exception: a throng of reporters and cameramen crowded in front of me like a firing squad, each pointing a camera in my direction. Emmanuel later estimated the media presence at between thirty and forty people, but through the field of my visor, it looked like a hundred. It was the largest opening-day media gathering I'd ever seen around our pits.

"Okay," I heard Richee say through my earplugs. "Lyn, you've got fifteen gallons of fuel. Go out and have a good run. We'll do a systems check when you get in."

"Got it," I said. Fifteen gallons was enough methanol for about ten laps. I was only supposed to run three or four, at the most five laps, then bring it in for the cameras. Of course, if things went well . . .

"Okay, kiddo," Dick said through the microphone on his headset. "Go out and have a good run. Stay out as long as you want. Just get comfortable and let me know how the car is handling." He patted my helmet as he finished. There was nothing I could say. I just gave Dick and the crew the thumbs-up and prepared myself for another turn around this track I'd known and loved for so long.

Gary attached the starter to the rear of the car. When the track went green and the crew pushed me off and cleared the wheels, I pressed the throttle, becoming the first driver on the track for the 2001 Month of May.

"Looking good, Lyn," I heard Richee say on the radio. By the back stretch I had already moved past 150 mph, and I had no intention of slowing down. They might be ceremonial laps to some, but it was my butt in the seat of that race car, and nothing is ceremonial when you're driving at those kinds of speeds.

I would love to say that a flood of fond memories washed through my brain as I made this momentous final trip around Indy, but that would be a lie. I was in the moment, as you have to be when driving. I didn't intend to screw up my last laps in an Indy car with melancholy recollections of years gone by. The slightest hiccup and I could be in the wall. What a retirement that would have been!

When I crested the apex of Turn Four and shot onto the front straightaway I was traveling at well over 160 mph and getting faster by the second. I wasn't going to endanger the car or do anything stupid, but I wasn't going to putter around this thing, either. They wanted to know what the car felt like at speed, and that's exactly the kind of info I planned to give them.

"The car feels great," I said on the radio after coming out of Turn Two in my first full lap. And it did! The car felt solid, responded to the steering input, entered the corners well, and remained stable through throttle changes. I had confidence entering the turns, which allowed me to stay in the throttle through the apex of the turns. It felt great. Every bump on this old track felt wonderful. I even enjoyed the burning sensation in my nostrils from the methanol.

As I turned my second full lap at 181 mph, Dick had meandered down to the yard of bricks where Tony George was waiting with an ESPN camera crew and even more still photographers than the group that had seen me off.

"I thought she was just going to run a couple of warm-up laps," Tony said to Dick.

Dick shrugged and smiled. "I guess it depends on how you define 'warm-up.'"

I defined it as anything around the 200 mph mark. If I could get the car up to speed, I could save the crew a lot of man-hours by giving them good feedback before the team attempted to qualify. After all, getting the car in the race was the goal. If my little show could help Dick achieve that goal, then I was ready to do what was needed.

Suddenly I heard the words I dreaded over the headset. "Yellow flag, yellow flag," Richee called over the radio as I entered Turn Three. Scott Sharp—the driver who went on to win the pole position for the race—had blown an engine, and the yellow caution flag had come out.

"Coming in," I said. "I'm coming in."

"Roger that, Lyn. They're waiting for you at the start-finish line. Watch your speed in the pits and bring it in."

They were, indeed, waiting for me. The moment I stopped the car on the yard of bricks, what looked like a hundred flashbulbs popped as photographers engulfed the nose of the car. The crew was there to help me out, and Tony George was off to the side, waiting to accept my helmet. But Dick was the first person I saw.

He leaned over and put his hand on my shoulder. "Great job, kiddo," Dick said. "You did good."

As simple as they were, those were the words that meant the most to me. They summed up my entire Indy racing experience, a decade of my life in the greatest motor sporting event in the world. "Yep," I said to myself. "Great job. You did good."

PIT STOP

A second ago is gone, and a second from now might be. Now is all you've got. Go for it!

One happy driver after qualifying for my seventh Indy 500.
Photo: Courtesy of William J. Ray/Photo by Ray

After I raced in the Indy 500, two things happened that I never expected: I received many heartfelt letters and requests asking me for advice on how they or their daughters could also race in the Indy 500 as well as so much support from the fans and people in the Indianapolis community that I wanted to find a way I could give back, especially to girls.

So I established the Lyn St. James Foundation in December 1993. It's a 501 (c) 3 nonprofit educational organization that focuses on worldwide activities and programs for automotive safety and driver development, especially for women who aspire to become race car drivers.

The mission of the LSJ Foundation is to provide leadership, vision, resources, and financial support in order to create an open environment for women's growth in automotive fields. To date we have trained over 150 women drivers from

38 states and two countries through our driver development program and contributed to Girls, Inc., the Wilbur Shaw Soap Box Derby Hill in Indianapolis, and other charitable organizations; we have also donated numerous autographed items for various charities around the world.

The foundation envisions a future that includes equal opportunity and a genuine appreciation of women's accomplishments and contributions to society. For more information on the Lyn St. James Foundation or to find out how you can help, please check out my website, www.lynstjames.com, or write:

> The Lyn St. James Foundation
> 57D Gasoline Alley
> Indianapolis, IN 46222